A Haunting In Virginia

Larry Wilson

Copyright © 2020 Larry Wilson
First Edition: May 2020
All rights reserved.
ISBN-13: 978-1-7334631-1-9

ACKNOWLEDGEMENTS

To my family, friends and colleagues for their patience during the completion of the writing of this book. A special thank you to Adam, and Jessica Stock for sharing their haunting experiences and for allowing me to investigate and experience the strangeness for myself.

Contents

	Acknowledgements
7	Dedication
9	Prologue
16	Dr. Ugs
21	A Step Back in Time
21	History
22	Tragedy
28	**Haunting Stories**
31	The Rolling Ball
31	Donald the Ghost Boy
34	Footsteps from Nowhere
35	The Man in Black
37	First Sighting
38	Second Sighting
39	Third Sighting
40	The Boy in the Kitchen
41	Lights Turning On
44	Toy Stories
45	The Doll
47	The Wand
48	Ghost Dog
55	Hayden
57	The Woman's Voice

58	Boy in the Bathroom
59	Doors Closing and Locking on their Own
61	Poltergeist Activity
63	The Man in the Mirror
65	**Investigator's Personal Experience**
70	**EVP Evidence**
102	**Weighing the Evidence**
104	**Who Haunts the Building**
104	**Ghost Children**
106	**Male Ghost**
109	**Female Ghost**
110	**Psychic Evidence**
111	**Ghost Dog**
114	**Epilogue**
118	**Campfire Tales Extra**
119	**Paranormal Witness**
119	**Strangers in the Night**
122	**The House on Big Bend Road**
124	**The Villa Road House**
126	**About the Author**
128	**Books by Larry Wilson**

DEDICATION

This book is dedicated to all who have experienced the strangeness that the supernatural and the unexplained have to offer. To my colleagues looking for answers to the mysterious and spectacular questions that the paranormal presents us.

Larry Wilson

Prologue

This book is an account of a remarkable chain of unexplained events which took place in a small West Central, Illinois town and the evidence, from a series of investigations I conducted alone, from October 2017 to April 2019.

The investigations have produced the most significant and unparalleled audio evidence I have recorded in my nineteen-year career as a paranormal investigator.

During my investigations, I found a great deal of activity seemed to be taking place right under my nose, hidden from visible sight, detectable only by my investigative equipment.

The family living there came to believe that the building is haunted. Not by one, but several ghostly entities, including a ghost boy, a shadowy male figure referred to as the man in black and a ghost dog.

The building, in question, is on the town square, in the small but quaint town of Virginia, Illinois. At the crossroads of routes 125 and 78 in the heart of Cass County, Virginia is the county seat and is a mere forty miles from the state's capitol, Springfield.

Oh, did I mention that the building once housed a funeral home.

If you were to asked one of the many locals what they see as they drive by this marvelous old landmark, traveling from one place to the next, you would be met with laughter and a response that, there is nothing to see, other than an old building made of bricks and mortar.

But if you stop by to inspect as I have, you might discover that in the shadows and crevices of the old building, there is much more to see than mere bricks and mortar.

That there is a hidden world, untouched and invisible from sight, that intermingles with the living and if you are lucky or unlucky enough, as the case may be, you might even come face to face with one of the ghostly entities that roams about the building.

The account you are about to read is true, I know this, because I witnessed some of the strangeness that takes place, firsthand.

I believe the phantom voices and sounds that I recorded in the middle of the night, are paranormal, because there was no one else in the building for my equipment to record.

Not only did I record the strangeness, I believe that on April 17, 2019; I saw one of the ghostly beings that roams about in the shadows of the building.

Besides what I witnessed and recorded, I found the eyewitness testimony of the family who lived through the haunting, to not only be convincing and compelling, but downright chilling.

In addition to reading about the accounts of the family, you will read about the encounters of others, who have experienced the strangeness that the building has to offer.

For those of you who are first-time readers of my books, I will give you a brief introduction as to who I am, what I do and why I do it.

My name is Larry Wilson and I am a former private investigator, turned paranormal investigator and author, who has been looking into the unexplained for over nineteen years now.

I am the guy that people call when they think the boogeyman may lurk in the shadows of their home or business, and many times they are right.

Unlike those who pull the covers up over their head when the paranormal shows up at their doorstep, I seek the things that go bump in the night, searching for answers as to what these ghostly things are and where they come from!

I have investigated the full gamut of the paranormal, from the mundane to the extreme, sometimes with a team of one or two investigators, but most times I investigate alone.

In the nineteen years that I have investigated the supernatural and the unexplained, I have experienced both the malevolent and the benevolent side of hauntings

For this reason, I do not treat my investigations as fun and games or a hobby, but with respect and is an endeavor I pursue with purpose and caution.

My first encounter with the paranormal was on September 8, 1966. The date is easy to remember, because the night of my experience was the debut of a cool new television show, Star Trek.

If you grew up in the 1960s like I did, with only three channels to watch, remembering the date of the debut of a television show is an easy task, but when you see something beyond the grasp of reality on the same night, you never forget it.

It was around 8:30 P.M. At the time I was living in Petersburg, Illinois. I remember that my mom was in the kitchen and my brother was doing homework. Dad was not home, as he was out visiting a friend.

Our living room was arranged with our sofa under a window. It faced the north and rested up against the wall.

I was bored, so I looked out the window, as I did on many nights. Climbing up on the sofa, I kneeled on one of the sofa cushions with my elbows on the back of the sofa, my chin resting on my interwoven fingers.

As a child of seven, I enjoyed looking out this window at night, to watch trains that would stop at a small depot on a hillside, about a mile north of our home at 604 North 4th Street.

It was dark, so I unclasp my interwoven fingers, cupping them to my face, to block the glare from the living room light, that was reflecting on the window.

Pressing my nose against the glass to see outside, I remember the night as if it was yesterday. As soon as I looked out the window, I could see the stars, as it was a clear fall evening.

I noticed how large and strange the moon looked. It was the biggest and brightest moon that I had ever seen. The color was a strange and vibrant orange, and its shape was perfectly round.

I looked at the bright orange moon for several minutes. Its round shape and orange color mesmerized me. Then, something caught my attention.

Glancing toward my left or northwest, and looking higher in the night sky, I saw the bright yellow, crescent shape of the moon.

I glanced back at the orange object which I had thought was the moon and then looked back at the actual moon.

The moon was much smaller than the other object. The strange light appeared to be about the size of a half-dollar in the sky. One thing I will never forget about the object, is how perfectly round it was.

I continued staring at it, as if it hypnotized me. I couldn't take my eyes off of it. After several minutes, it sped off at a high rate of speed and shot off toward the northeast, before coming to an abrupt halt.

It was now half the size that it had been moments before. Then once again, it shot off at a high rate of speed and came to a sudden stop. It repeated this behavior one more time, before it sped up and disappeared into the northern sky.

Over the course of the next few weeks, something strange happened to me. I developed a clairvoyance or foreknowledge, that even as a seven-year-old boy, realized was not normal.

Sudden thoughts and premonitions would come to me and the next thing that I knew, the visions would occur.

It was not something that happened all the time, but when it did, I would get an uneasy feeling that something wasn't right. The thought would come to me and the next thing I knew, before the day was over, it would manifest itself into reality.

One example of this occurred when I had a vision that a train would hit someone. In my vision I saw a four-door white car, being hit by a train, on the railroad crossing at the intersection where our house was.

Later that evening, I was lying on my parent's bed, staring out our south window. I could hear the train whistle blowing and could tell that it was nearby.

Next, I heard a car speed up and when I turned my head toward the east, saw the neighbor lady who lived around the corner from our house speeding toward the railroad crossing in her white four-door car trying to beat the train. It was the same scenario that I envisioned a few hours before.

As I watched, the train struck the rear end of the car. The woman driver sustained injuries that resulted in her being taken to the hospital.

On another occasion, I was in school when the village fire alarm sounded. I looked over at one of my classmates and had the strange feeling that it was his house on fire.

I remember hearing him say, *"I sure hope it's not my house."* Later that afternoon, family members came to the school to pick him up, because it had, in fact, been his house that had caught fire.

After about two months, the visions stopped. But even as a child, I recognized what was happening to me was peculiar. I believe the premonitions and strange light that I saw on September 8 were connected. But if they were, then what did I see that night.

Was it extraterrestrial or supernatural? Was it closer to me than I realized and through some telepathy, opened up my psychic awareness?

Was I caught up in a residual energy field by something from another world or dimension? If so, was it by accident or did something intelligent know I was there and could see me, and as a result affected me.

I hope someone who reads this book, and who lived in the Petersburg area may have also witnessed the same event. If so, I wonder if they experienced premonitions like I did.

In the summer of 2010, I attended a paranormal consortium in Springfield, Illinois. I was explaining what I had seen as a child in 1966, to the Illinois Mutual UFO Network (MUFON) director, Sam Maranto.

As I explained my story, Sam would nod in an affirming manner, as if to say, *"Yes, I have heard a similar story before."* After I finished telling my story, Sam said. *"Larry, did you ever think when you saw the object speeding up at a high rate of speed, that maybe it wasn't traveling like you thought? What if I told you, that I believe you witnessed a wormhole in space, an inter-dimensional portal? Instead of it moving in the manner that you thought, what if when you saw the object getting smaller, you were seeing the wormhole closing up?"*

What Sam said made sense to me, and the more I thought about it, the more I agreed with his theory.

Because of this childhood experience, I developed an interest in mystery and adventure and pursued a career as a private investigator. I worked over a decade as a P.I. and my training and experience has been invaluable to me as a paranormal investigator.

The reason I write books about my adventures is not to convince people that ghost, and supernatural things are real, because that is not possible. You have to see and experience the things I write about, firsthand, to know if they exist.

I write books to go on record and document the things I witness. For me, I believe, because I have seen these things with my own eyes and have witnessed many of the fascinating and sometimes terrifying things that the supernatural has to offer.

After reading this book, I suspect that you will agree that the world, is much bigger and stranger than we have been led to believe and not all that is out there can be explained by the science and logic, that we were taught in school.

But suppose one day, you are plunged into a world where the ghostly things that you read about appear right in front of you, without warning.

This, my friends, is what happened to the Stock family of Virginia, Illinois, after moving into a former funeral home.

I assure you, if they didn't believe in ghost and hauntings before moving into the property at 142 East Beardstown Street, they do now.

Because as they say, *"Seeing is believing!"*

DR. UGS

The Storefront

If you ask most people if they believe in ghost, they will answer, no.

But if you asked them, if they would spend the night in a haunted house alone, more than likely they would refuse based on fear.

But why fear something if it doesn't exist?

Many people share in this indecision for ghosts and ghostly things, for the simple reason, there is no way to prove they don't exist. So, why take a chance if you don't have to.

If one doesn't believe in ghost, why then, do ghost stories and movies of such things, frighten so many?

To best answer this question, I quote the well-known science fiction author, H. P. Lovecraft, who once said. *"The oldest and strongest emotion of mankind is fear, and the oldest and strongest kind of fear is fear of the unknown."*

Or to quote President Franklin Delano Roosevelt, from his famous 1933 inaugural speech, *"We have nothing to fear but fear itself."*

If one were to characterize Dr. Ugs Drugstore Café in one sentence, the best description is, *"Good food, good drinks, good times, and ghosts."*

The description not only reflects the atmosphere and goings on at the forefront of this quaint small-town establishment, but also reflects what takes place behind the scenes.

If you ever get the chance to visit the café for dinner or to take in a performance by one of the talented musicians or comedians that often perform there, you might miss the real entertainment that performs behind the scenes.

I can't recall ever investigating as varied an assortment of unexplained things taking place, as at Dr. Ugs.

You will understand what I mean, after reading about the strange things that the current owners and others have experienced. Some are not only mysterious, but downright chilling.

The building is a throwback to the days of yesteryear. The first time that I walked into Dr. Ugs in the fall of 2017, it reminded me of the old Long Branch Saloon, where, as a kid, I would watch my favorite TV Western heroes hang out on the television show, Gunsmoke.

All that was missing was Marshall Dillon, his deputy Festus Haggen, Sam the bartender and the establishment's owner, Miss Kitty.

When I arrived, husband and wife owners, Adam and Jessica Stock greeted me. Not only is 142 East Beardstown Street their place of business, it is their home, as the couple live above the business in a beautiful loft style apartment, with their daughters Corinna, age seven and Ella, three.

If you are wondering about the name of the business. The previous owners and founders, Mike and Susan Carson named the establishment, *Dr. Ugs.*

They were stumped for a name for the business. So, since the building housed several drug stores over the years, and the sign on the facing of the building still read, DRUGS. They added a period after the letter *"R"* in Drug*s* and named the business, DR. UGS.

I first met Adam a few weeks prior at their Dr. Ugs Café located inside *The Hand of Fate Microbrewery,* in my hometown of Petersburg, Illinois, just a short thirty-minute drive northeast of Virginia.

It was while attending a reunion of sorts with some of my old baseball teammates from the 1970s, 80s and 90s.

Other than family and friends, my two passions in life are exploring the paranormal and baseball, the greatest sport invented, which I played for thirty-six years.

I have fond memories and made many good friends playing sandlot baseball.

One such friend is my old teammate Bob Roodhouse, who is Adam's uncle, and was visiting from the Seattle, Washington area.

As the evening progressed, my conversation with Bob turned to my interest in the paranormal and writing books about the many experiences I have had.

It is a mixed bag when I tell people I am a paranormal investigator. Their reactions range from very interested, all the way to, *"This guy is crazy."*

Bob is fair-minded, and when he found out I am a paranormal researcher, he said.

"You should meet my nephew Adam; he and his wife Jessica are the owners of Dr. Ugs Cafe. They have a second location in Virginia and live above the business.

The place is a former funeral home and from what they have told me, is haunted as hell."

Because of our conversation, later that evening, Bob introduced me to Adam, and as they say, the rest is history.

Adam was very cordial and straightforward and seemed to be open to discussing the goings on at the Virginia location.

After Bob explained that I was a paranormal investigator and the reason for introducing me, Adam was not only open to talking about what was taking place but was open to an investigation.

Unfortunately for me, the restaurant was busy with customers and Adam needed to get back to work, so we cut our conversation short, before I arranged a time and place to continue our talk and schedule the investigation. I also failed to get Adams phone number to set up such a meeting.

The following day, I kept thinking about the prospect of investigating an ongoing haunting at a former funeral home.

The last building that I investigated that had housed a morgue was the old Norb Andy's Tavern in nearby Springfield.

Not only did I record several fascinating disembodied voices there, I witnessed a chilling event that I still think about to this day. I will discuss what happened that night a bit later in the book.

Not wanting to miss out on the opportunity to investigate the building, I sent a Facebook message to Bob and asked him for Adams contact information.

Bob supplied the information, so I phoned Adam.

We had a brief discussion in which Adam indicated that he told his wife Jessica about our conversation in Petersburg. She was excited at the prospect of having someone come out and try to document the strange things they had been experiencing.

Later that same afternoon, I received a phone call from Jessica, and we scheduled a date and time for me to come out to do a pre-investigation interview and walkthrough of the building.

A Step Back in Time

History and Tragedy

History

Built in 1854 as a wooden structure, the two-story brick, 10,000 plus square foot building with full basement, was destroyed in 1896, when fire burned the whole south side of the square.

The building was rebuilt in 1897 using an Eastlake style architecture, a style fundamental to the late Victorian period in terms of antique furniture classifications and is part of the Queen Anne style of Victorian architecture.

A well-known Eastlake style house, which seems fitting to the Dr. Ugs Café haunting, is one in Los Angeles, California at 1330 Carroll Avenue.

The house was used in the Michael Jackson music video, Thriller. So, as you can see, Eastlake architecture seems quite fitting for a haunted building.

The Dr. Ugs building has been the location for many thriving enterprises, including three funeral homes.

The J. E. King company sold pianos and furniture and served as an undertaking establishment and is one of the first known businesses at the location.

Purnell Funeral Services and the Virgin and Dodd's Furniture Store and Funeral Home were in the building in the 1920s.

Hopping Drug Store occupied the building in the 1930s, and records show that a Dr. Snow had his dentist office on the second floor of the building in what is now the Stocks, kitchen and dining room.

Other businesses included Dougherty Drugs, Finney Drugs and in more recent years, Southside and the Phoenix bar.

Tragedy

Not all the building's history has been pleasant.

In 1929, there was a tragic death by shooting that occurred in front of the building, which involved an employee of the Virgin and Dodd's funeral home.

The death may shed some light on the ghostly activity that takes place today and may also explain an EVP that I recorded during my first investigation of the building, on Halloween night 2017.

The following is from the State Journal Register Newspaper and describes the 1929 incident.

State Journal Newspaper
February 18, 1929

KILLS ENEMY IN FRONT OF VIRGINIA STORE
Victim Dies in St. John's Hospital, Assailant to Face Murder Charge

(Virginia, Feb 18)

A longstanding personal feud blazed today to leave James Potter, 54, utility man in a local undertaking establishment, dead in St. John's Hospital, Springfield, with three bullets in his left breast, and Charles Davis attendant at the White Rock gas station, Virginia, jailed on the charge of murder.

The shooting happened at 1:15 o'clock in the afternoon, in front of the doorway of the Virgin and Dodd's' furniture store and undertaking establishment where Potter worked.

Standing less than four feet from Potter, Davis is alleged to have pulled the .38 caliber revolver he was carrying as a gas station attendant and fired three times.

Died At 8:10 P.M.

He was taken to St. John's Hospital where his condition was so serious, doctors would not risk an operation to remove the bullets. He died at 8:10 o'clock. Davis remained at the scene of the shooting and was placed under arrest by Deputy Sheriff Arthur Reynolds.

The two men, living within less than half a block of each other on North Morgan street, were alleged to have been at odds for several years. Nature of the trouble between the two is not known, although the old row is claimed to have led to today's altercation.

Last Saturday afternoon the body of George Webb, Davis' brother-in-law who died in Hammond, Indiana, was to be buried from the Davis home here.

Davis is alleged to have called up the undertakers in charge and stated that he did not want Potter to be sent out to the funeral, "because of old troubles."

This afternoon, arming himself with an ice pick, Potter went over to the gasoline station where Davis worked and is alleged to have forced the attendant to accompany him to the undertaking parlor to apologize.

Engaged in Argument

The two entered the establishment where they engaged in a heated argument.

Alfred Dodd's, junior partner of the firm was present and finally told the men: "Get outside if you want to settle your differences."

The two men walked out, and as they stood in the doorway, Davis is alleged to have pulled out his pistol and shot three times. He made no effort to escape. Davis had a permit to carry a pistol while on duty as attendant at the station.

Inquest will be conducted by Coroner Ernest Dye, according to statement made last night. The investigation will take several days, and inquest cannot be held until he has arranged with Myron Mills, States Attorney of Cass County, for the appearances of witnesses.

Potter is survived by his wife, Ella and five children, Lois, Willard, Jane, James and Catherine. (End)

A follow-up newspaper article of February 21, 1929 showed that a coroner's jury failed to agree on a verdict and a new inquest would be necessary.

A further newspaper article, dated March 21, 1929, showed that a *"No true bill"* was returned against Charles Davis, in connection to the James Potter shooting.

For those not familiar with the legal term, *"No true Bill."* It is a legal procedure to dismiss charges against a defendant when the grand jury does not find enough evidence to charge them with violating a law.

As you will read later in the book, on Halloween night of 2017, while alone in the building, I recorded an EVP that may relate to the James Potter shooting incident of 1929.

EVP, stands for *"Electronic Voice Phenomena."* Which are voices and sounds that come from an unknown source and recorded by audio recorders.

Many times, the voices and sounds recorded are not heard by investigators, which was the case in 2017.

Most in the paranormal field believe that the voices recorded are disembodied voices of the dead, while others believe that the voices come from other dimensions and realms.

Research of local history shows that James Potter was not the only Potter family member involved in a gun battle in the small town of Virginia.

The first was when William Potter shot B.F. Perrine in 1888. William and James were brothers.

I could not determine through a search of historical records, whether Charles Davis was related to B.F. Perrine or connected to the feud that the Potters had with Perrine.

(Authors note: The name Perrine is spelled both, "Perrine and Perrin," in newspaper archives.)

Daily Illinois State Journal
November 24, 1888
Virginia, Illinois

Shot by a Bus Driver

At about 9 o'clock this morning, William Potter, a man of about 33 years old, employed by H.H. Turner as bus driver, walked from his home to a blacksmith shop, which is situated on the corner of an adjoining lot, and finding the smith, B.F. Perrin, standing talking to a friend.

He pulled out a number 32-caliber revolver and fired three shots in rapid succession, each ball taking effect.

The first ball entered the shoulder above the heart, ranging down, and lodged below the shoulder blade at the back. The second entered the groin, going clean through. The third struck the right hand and came out the back of the wrist.

Dr. C.M. Hubbard was called and extracted the ball in the back and dressed his wound. He pronounced the wounds not necessarily fatal but considered the case a very critical one.

The cause of the affair is an old feud existing between the two families. They have been quarreling back and forth all summer.

Potter, who made no attempt to get away, was immediately arrested and lodged in jail to await the results of Perrin's wounds.

Daily Illinois State Journal
November 26, 1888
Virginia Illinois (Special)

The Cass County Shooting

Wm. Potter, the omnibus driver who shot B.F. Perrin here Saturday morning, as a result of an old feud between the families of the two men, will have his preliminary examination tomorrow morning. A relative of Potter's is on the ground as believed for the purpose of going bail for Potter.

Perrin, though shot in three places, is doing well and will, it is thought, soon recover, so that Potter will, in all probability, be held to bail, unless an unfavorable change in Perrin's condition should develop.

Daily Illinois State Journal
November 27, 1888
Virginia Illinois (Special)

Perrin Out of Danger-Potter's Preliminary Trial Today

The Virginia Shooting Case

Wm. Potter, who shot B.F. Perrine last Saturday morning, is in jail awaiting the results of Perrine's injuries. He will probably have a preliminary examination Wednesday, as Perrine is now considered out of danger. Sympathy of the public is with Potter, who is a cripple and quite ineffective. (End)

(Authors note.) One odd if not eerie coincidence that I came across during the search of records on the building, is that James Potters wife's name is Ella, which is also the name of Adam and Jessica's youngest daughter. Since the year 1910 the name Ella is ranked as the 140th most popular girls name or 0.172 percent of girl's born in the

United States. Unfortunately, there is no way to determine if this is coincidence or fate, but I find it interesting, nonetheless.

Haunting Stories

For me personally, the most compelling evidence of the haunting at Dr. Ugs, are the stories that the Stock family and others tell of their experiences in the building.

Stories of strangeness that sound more like something that you would read in a book by Edgar Allan Poe, Washington Irving or the scare master himself, Stephen King.

I arrived for the pre-investigation and interview at 7:00 P.M. and was greeted by Adam and his wife Jessica.

Both come from small towns and are very down to earth, straightforward people, which for me, added to the credibility of their accounts of the paranormal activity that they experienced.

Not to mention, their generosity which didn't hurt matters either, as they treated me to a couple pints of delicious cream ale, brewed by the Hand of Fate Microbrewery in Petersburg, which quenched my thirst as we chatted about the ghostly activity taking place.

Befitting for such a loving couple as Adam and Jessica, they married on Valentine's day, 2010, although it may have been just as fitting if they had selected Halloween, as their experiences in the Virginia building, are not their first brush with the paranormal.

Early in their married life, they lived in a house in Greenview, Illinois that had been vacant for some thirty years.

The last people to live in the house before the Stock's purchased the home were a husband and wife couple, who died in a car accident years ago, on New Year's Eve.

Jessica told me that there was something odd about the Greenview house that made you feel that you were not alone, and it always seemed to have a different feel about it, around the New Year's holiday.

"It was more than just knowing that they died on New Year's Eve," Jessica said. *"The house just seemed creepy around that time of the year."*

As a child, Jessica lived in a house on the outskirts of Greenview, where she had several otherworldly experiences that she couldn't explain. One such experience entailed seeing the ghost of a woman in her bedroom. Her experiences are personal, so I won't elaborate on what she saw, but the stories she told me have led me to believe that Jessica is sensitive to the spirit world.

Adam agrees with my assessment and has seen her ability in action several times since they have been married.

Her apparent sensitivity to the spirit world may explain some of the ghostly activity she has witnessed at the Virginia location.

I base my presumption on something that a psychic colleague told me early in my career as a paranormal investigator.

My colleague explained that I should be certain, that seeking spirits and delving into the supernatural is something that I wanted to pursue.

Because as she forewarned. *"If a spirit is trying to contact our world from the other side, who better to communicate with than someone who is sensitive to spirits, or a paranormal investigator like you Larry, who is trying to record their voices."*

She further explained that, *"At some point, if you continue to delve into the supernatural, you won't have to go looking for spirits, because they will come looking for you."*

Well, she was one hundred percent accurate, because my wife and I have been married for thirty-five years and have lived at three different locations. We have lived in our current home since 1994 and had nothing strange or unusual take place at the locations we lived. Nothing, that is, until I began investigating the paranormal.

Since then, we have seen and heard things in our home that neither of us can explain, things like hearing breaking glass and heavy objects falling. But after exhaustive searches, we can never find the source of the commotion.

Not only have we heard noises, but we have witnessed a full-bodied phantom that we call the *"Thin Boy,"* on three separate occasions.

We named him the *"Thin Boy"* because of his appearance, which is that of a short, thin, teenage boy, with shoulder-length brown hair, who always wears black and gray clothes.

The strangest thing about him is that he is not ghostly, but appears as a solid human being, always hiding his face.

So, it is possible that the ghostly things that roam the Virginia building act up, because they know that Jessica can sense their presence and may see and hear them.

Not only is Jessica sensitive to spirits, but based on the stories the couple told me, it is also possible that their children are sensitive to spirits as well.

The renowned Psychic and author, James Van Praagh believes that many children are what he calls, touched by spirit.

"It's not unusual for small children to be aware of spirits around them," Praagh states in his online blog. *"They seem to be sensitive to energy and can share insights and wisdom far beyond their years."*

As you continue, you will read one such story about Corinna, the Stock's oldest daughter, that seems to reflect Van Praagh's statement.

After living in the Greenview house and aware of Jessica's sensitivity to spirits, Adam was more than apprehensive at the thought of moving into a former funeral home.

"I thought about it a lot," Adam said. *"I remember, thinking to myself that I must be out of my mind moving into an old funeral home!"*

Well, as the old saying goes, *"Hindsight is twenty-twenty."* Because, in April 2012, the Stock's bought the building and existing restaurant from Mike and *Susan* Carson and a short time later, moved into the building.

It didn't take long before Adam, and Jessica experienced the strangeness that the building offered.

The Rolling Ball

"It all began in July 2012, the very first night that we stayed in the building," Adam explained.

"It was in the middle of the night. Jessica and I were sleeping on the floor, because we had just moved in and didn't have our bed set up yet. Everything was quiet, when out of the blue Jessica and I were startled awake by a loud noise. It sounded like someone had dropped a billiard ball, which was followed by the sound of something rolling across the wooden floor. We got up and searched for the source of the noise but found nothing that could have caused the sound that we heard. It was crazy."

To this day, neither Adam nor Jessica have been able to determine what caused the mysterious sound and it has not happened again.

Donald the Ghost Boy

One of the more chilling stories that the Stock's told me occurred later that year, in the fall of 2012. I have heard a lot of stories from clients over the years, but this story is one of the more memorable ones that I have been told.

The incident took place upstairs in the Stock's living quarters. It was late afternoon, and everything was normal, or so it seemed.

Their oldest daughter, Corinna, was two and a half and was a short distance away playing and amusing herself in a small tent in her playroom.

"She was just learning to talk and rarely said anything when playing alone," Jessica said.

"Plus, it was unusual that Corinna had been playing for so long without coming to see what Adam and I were doing. We were nearby, when we heard Corinna talking. She wasn't talking gibberish either, it was like she was carrying on a conversation with someone." Jessica continued.

"I remember Adam and I looking at each other dumbfounded by what we were hearing. Because like I said, she was just learning to talk, let alone forming sentences."

Surprised by what they were hearing, Adam and Jessica stopped what they were doing and decided they had better go check on Corinna.

As they neared the play tent, they could still hear Corinna talking as if she was conversing with someone. So, Jessica asked Corinna to step out of the tent for a minute, which she did.

When the young parents asked Corinna who she was talking to, little did they expect the shocking answer they were about to receive.

"I'm talking to my friend Donald." Corinna replied. *"He's the little boy who sucks his fingers and is looking for his mama."*

Next and without hesitation, Corinna showed how her invisible playmate sucked his fingers, by placing the first two fingers of her hand into her mouth.

"What she did next was chilling," Jessica said, to which Adam agreed.

Jessica explained that Corinna was standing in front of and facing them as she told them about her friend Donald.

Then, she suddenly stopped talking, leaned toward her right and peeked around her parents, as if she was looking at someone.

After a moment, she straightened back up and said. *"But I'm not supposed to tell anyone."*

Adam said that he and Jessica looked at each other in disbelief, because it appeared someone was coaching their daughter from behind them, except there was no one there.

"That sent a cold chill down my spine!" Adam said. *"Especially when in the back of your mind, you know you're living in a place that is a former funeral home."*

Even more puzzling to the Stock's was how Corinna came up with the name Donald, because they didn't know anyone by this name, that Corina would know, nor could they recall any of the kid's shows that she watched, having a character named Donald.

Not to mention, she was too little to make up such a story.

The incident in the fall of 2012 was the one and only time that Corinna would mention Donald, her invisible playmate. Is this because she has never seen him again?

Or is it because her phantom friend instructed her not to say anything?

Whoever the little boy is, Corrina was not afraid of him and seemed to think that he was just another child to play with.

As you will read later in the chapter, there are two other eyewitness accounts involving the ghostly activity of a little boy.

In addition, during several of my investigations, I recorded the voice of a child that may be from the phantom boy.

Footsteps from Nowhere

For some reason, Corinna, didn't like to sleep in her own bed, and most nights the Stock's would hear the pitter-patter of the sound of their daughter's footsteps, as she hurried from her bedroom, to the safety and comfort of her parents' bed.

This happened so often, that the couple expected it, and instead of fussing and trying to get Corinna to go back to her room, they would pick her up and put her in bed with them, so that everyone could get a good night's sleep.

One particular night, the sound of the footsteps scurrying across the wooden floor and heading toward their bedroom awakened Adam.

Figuring that Corinna was making her mad dash to their room, he rolled over and reached out to lift the little girl into bed.

But to Adam's surprise, when he rolled over and reached out to grab Corinna, no one was there. Shocked by what had happened, Adam turned over to wake Jessica, but when he did, furthering his bewilderment, he saw Corinna sound asleep next to Jessica.

"It was the darndest thing," Adam said. *"I know what I heard, because it woke me up. It sounded just like Corinna running into our room. I'm positive it wasn't the building settling; it was little footsteps. It shocked me when I reached down to pick Corrina up and no one was there."*

The Stock's told me they understood why Corinna didn't like to sleep in her room. Because there was something about that part of the upstairs that gave them both an uncomfortable feeling. So much so, that Jessica spent a night alone in Corinna's bed, while her daughter slept with Adam.

"I couldn't sleep, there was something about the room," she said. *"It gave me a creepy feeling. I just wanted out of there."*

Not long after Jessica spent the night in Corinna's bedroom, they moved their daughter's bedroom to the room just north of theirs. What was once Corinna's bedroom is now the playroom. After moving her, Corinna began sleeping through the night.

The Man in Black

Adam and Jessica have both seen a shadowy figure that they call the *Man in Black*.

Jessica has seen him point blank on two occasions, and Adam has seen him once out of the corner of his eyes.

Although they refer to him as the *Man in Black,* I believe what they have seen, is better known in a paranormal sense as a *Shadow Man*.

Most of you, who have an interest in the paranormal, are familiar with the term *Shadow Person or Shadow Man*. But for those of you who are not, here is the Cliff's Notes explanation of what I believe them to be.

A *Shadow Man* is a three-dimensional ambiguous silhouette, resembling the shadow of a person. They don't seem to be the cast shadow of a person or some supernatural being, but are their own independent life force, resembling the silhouette of a person.

Other characteristics, reported by witnesses, are that the shadow creatures are very tall and are much darker than the obscure shadows they come out of.

Some say that these mysterious figures seem to be oblivious to their surroundings, while other reports would lead one to believe that they knew the witness was there.

There are various theories as to the origin of these mysterious figures, ranging from spirits of the dead, Tulpa's, which are thought forms, demons and interdimensional beings.

As a paranormal investigator, I not only believe shadow people exist; I have witnessed one with my own eyes. This occurred while investigating the well-known and very haunted, Farrar School, in Iowa.

The incident transpired in the fall of 2013 when I took a local radio station's morning show host with me to record our annual Halloween show.

Nancy Oliver, the owner of the building, gave us a tour of the location prior to the investigation. During the tour, she told a story about a seven-foot-tall shadow man that roams the building.

She showed us an artist's rendition of the shadowy figure, drawn by one witness. When Nancy told the story, I wasn't sure that I believed it.

That night, while I was setting up surveillance cameras, and was hooking up the fourth and final infrared camera to the DVR and monitor, I noticed movement on the monitor coming from camera three, which I had set up in the school's gymnasium.

When I looked at the monitor, I couldn't believe my eyes.

What I saw was a tall, three-dimensional silhouette of a man, that was darker than the pitch-black shadowy corners of the gymnasium. It wasn't a cast shadow on the wall, mind you, because it was walking in front of the bleachers that were against the gym wall.

It was swinging its arms like the bigfoot creature in the old Patterson-Gimlin film from 1967, as it walked across the floor like it didn't have a care in the world.

Using an object hanging on the wall behind the bleachers for visual reference, this thing had to be at least seven-feet-tall, if not taller.

It appeared to have a potbelly and was wearing a short-brimmed cap that reminded me of the type that an old sea-captain would wear.

Unfortunately, when I saw it, I hadn't started the surveillance cameras recording. Not having the cameras recording is my biggest regret in the nineteen years that I have been investigating the paranormal. Because if I could see it on the monitor, I would have recorded it.

First Sighting

The first person to see the *Man in Black* was Jessica, in the fall of 2012.

When the family first moved in, their sofa was under the west window, in what is now Adam and Jessica's bedroom. It was around 3:30 P.M., and Jessica was sitting on the sofa, waiting for Adam to come home from work.

While waiting for Adam, a sudden feeling of uneasiness came over her as though someone was there. Then, without warning, she heard someone stomping their feet as though they were angry.

Her first thought was that Adam was home and was in a bad mood.

When she looked up, Jessica couldn't believe her eyes, because she saw who or what was making the noise.

The following is her description of what she saw.

"When I looked up, I saw the dark figure of a man; it was about the same height as Adam, only its shoulders were broader than his. Everything about him was black, he didn't appear to be a ghost, because he wasn't transparent like you would expect a ghostly figure to be. He was wearing a high collar black coat, that was long and flowing and appeared draped over its body. He seemed upset or grumpy, and at first, I thought Adam had come home upset about something that happened at work. But the flowing coat and the fact that it simply vanished, made me realize that it wasn't Adam." Jessica said.

"I can't explain it, but I had this overwhelming feeling, that this man was furious about something."

She further explained that what she saw was three dimensional in appearance and was not a shadow cast on the wall. He or it, was walking down the hallway minding his own business, then disappeared.

Second Sighting

Adam was next to see the *Man in Black*. His encounter took place in the early winter of 2012. On the night in question, both Jessica and Corinna were out, so Adam was home alone.

"It was early evening, and I was taking a shower, in the large walk-in shower, on the east side of the loft." Adam said.

"The previous owners constructed the shower so that Susan's elderly father, could maneuver his wheelchair in and out of it. So, at the time of the incident, there wasn't a door on the shower." Adam explained.

"At first, I was facing the east and had my back toward the shower room entrance. At one point, I turned around facing the shower room doorway. As I turned, I glimpsed a dark figure, walk past the doorway, heading toward the south."

Thinking Jessica had returned home, Adam called out to her. *"Hey Jessica!"* But there was no answer.

"When Jessica didn't respond, the hair stood up on the back of my neck," Adam said. *"Because I know I saw someone walk by."*

Adam only glimpsed what went by, but he is certain, that he saw someone, or something, walk past the door.

One thing I have noticed in my investigations at Dr. Ugs, is that cars and car headlights do not cause shadows to appear to move at floor level on the east hallway.

The second story is too high for cars to cause the movement that both Adam and Jessica saw. When I have seen headlights reflecting upstairs, the lights have always been at or near the ceiling. Even shadows that are caused by light coming through the transoms are at ceiling level.

Third Sighting

Jessica was unsure of the day or month that she saw the ghostly figure the second time, but it was after Adam's encounter.

"I was upstairs doing laundry and was at the south end of the building near the elevator." Jessica began.

"I looked up and saw this man coming toward me. Unlike the first man that I saw in the fall, this thing, was white in appearance. I could see it was a man, who had a white collar and was wearing what looked like an old fashion top hat, that was also white."

Jessica continued. *"Not only was he walking in the same direction and path as before, he was walking toward me, but, before I had time to react, he vanished."*

Adam and Jessica are not sure if the three shadowy figures are the same, but their gut feeling is that they relate to each other.

Regardless, one question remains. Why are the shadowy figures only seen in the hallway, wandering the same path?

Research that the Stocks have done, may answer this question.

They discovered during their research, that years ago, there was a staircase where the elevator is located.

So, if the shadowy figures are spirits or ghostly remnants from the past, perhaps then, they at one time, used the back staircase and for some unknown reason are earthbound, still following the same path.

If this is the case, the logical question becomes, what is their connection to the building.

When I asked Jessica if it seemed like the shadowy figures were aware of her presence, she told me she didn't think so.

"It seemed like they were just passing through," She said. *"Minding their own business like I wasn't even there."*

Whoever the shadowy figures are will probably remain a mystery unless further records searches can turn up any clues to their identity.

The Boy in the Kitchen

I heard so many compelling stories during my interview with Adam and Jessica, that it is hard to pick out a favorite.

But the next incident I am about to tell you, is high up on the list.

It took place in 2013 and was witnessed by an employee who was the new cook at the restaurant. He no longer works for the Stocks, so for this story, I will refer to him as the cook and not by name.

The incident occurred during the morning hours before the restaurant opened. Jessica was working in the bar area a few feet from the cook, who was in the kitchen preparing things for the day.

At one point, the cook came out of the kitchen and approached Jessica with a concern. He said.

"Your little boy just ran through the kitchen again, so I thought I better tell you. I'm afraid he might hurt himself."

Surprised by what the cook said, Jessica looked at him and replied. *"We don't have a little boy, we have a little girl, and besides, she's not here right now."*

Dumbfounded by Jessica's response, he again explained to Jessica what he saw and returned to the kitchen.

(Authors note.) The night of July 3, 2018, I investigated the Dr. Ugs building for the third time. It was during this investigation that I recorded the voice of a small child. The voice sounded like a little boy, but when listening to recorded voices of children, it is hard to discern the gender.

The investigation was conducted alone, so no one else was in the building that I could have mistaken for the child's voice.

For this reason, I believe beyond any reasonable doubt, that the voice is a legitimate unexplained disembodied voice.

The voice calls out, *"Daddy,"* as if he is looking for his father. Could this be Donald, the boy Corinna was talking to who she said was looking for his mama? If so, is he also looking for his daddy as well?

Over the years, I have recorded the voices of children calling out for their mothers and fathers and it breaks my heart to think there is a spirit or soul of a lost child alone, wandering about, in search of their loved ones.

Some investigators would say that because it sounds like the voice of an innocent child, doesn't mean that it is. Rather, it could be the voice of a negative spirit or something much worse, trying to lure an investigator or unsuspecting family into believing that it is a child, when it is an entity with less than innocent intentions.

Based on my experiences in the last nineteen years, I sometimes agree with this assessment.

But this doesn't seem to be the case at Dr. Ugs, because the activity experienced in the building seems to be more of a benevolent nature, with no ill intent intended.

Lights Turning On

When Adam told me the story of how lights would turn on by themselves, my first thought was that they either had a bad light switch, or there was a short circuit in the wiring. I changed my mind, when Adam showed how the switch works, which invalidated my theory.

The light switch in question, controls three hanging ceiling lights in the main upstairs area of the residence and is on the east wall near the shower, in the area where the shadow man roams.

It is a *"rotary dimmer switch."* I'm sure most of you are familiar with dimmer switches, but just in case you are not, dimmer switches, turn lights on and off and also adjust the brightness of a light, with the lowest setting when turned all the way to the left and at full brightness when turned to the far right.

Most rotary dimmers have a push-on and off function where you have to push the dial straight in until it clicks to turn the light fixture on or off.

Others turn all the way to the left or right until they click to turn the lights on or off. The style of switch the Stocks have is the latter.

The incident I am about to describe, took place on a fall night in 2017. It was somewhere around three o'clock in the morning and the family was sound asleep in their beds.

Without warning, a bright light awoke Adam and Jessica. Sitting up in bed, the couple looked around and noticed that the overhead ceiling lights were on.

Not sure what was happening, Adam got out of bed and began scanning the upstairs with his eyes to make sure they didn't have an intruder.

"I know that I turned the lights off before going to bed," Adam told me. *"Because we never sleep with the lights on."*

Not seeing or hearing anything, he walked over to the light switch and turned the knob toward the left to turn it off, but when he did, it made a clicking sound.

Then it hit him. To turn the lights on or off, you have to rotate the knob past the on or off position, which clicks, locking the switch in the selected position.

So, the light could not have turned on by itself. Someone has to manipulate it.

Adam told me that the lights have turned on by themselves one other time, since the original incident. But if there was a faulty switch, one would think the lights would turn on by themselves more often than two times in the seven plus years they have lived in the building.

Another incident with the lighting occurred in August 2018, only this time, I was present when it happened.

I was presenting audio evidence from my July investigation to the Stock's in the downstairs restaurant area, when we noticed that one of the hanging ceiling lights, closest to the front of the restaurant, flickered on and off, each time I played back an audio recording for them.

This didn't occur occasionally during my evidence presentation, but each and every time that I played an audio clip for the Stocks.

The light wasn't flickering when I arrived and didn't start until I began playing the recordings.

Each time that I played an audio clip, without fail, the light flickered.

It was uncanny how the light worked fine until I played an audio clip.

I asked Adam if the light flickered before I came. He told me it had not and further explained that he had never noticed it flickering before.

When the presentation was over, the odd flickering stopped.

I hung around for another half an hour, talking to Adam and Jessica, and not once did it happen again.

Was the flickering light a sign from a spirit that it wanted our attention or perhaps was listening to the recording and trying to let us know that *"Hey, that's my voice you are listening to?"*

Since the incident, Adam has checked the light and found nothing wrong with it.

There is no way to know for sure who or what caused the light to flicker. But as of the writing of this book, the light has not flickered since.

Toy Stories

Do ghost children play with toys? Well, it seems to be the case at Dr. Ugs.

The first instance of a toy operating on its own occurred in the middle of the night, October 2017. Both Adam and Jessica witnessed the incident.

Their experience took place just a few days before my first investigation on Halloween night of that same year.

All was quiet, and everyone was sleeping when something woke, Adam and Jessica. It was the sound of a particular toy, turning on and off.

They recognized the sound to be that of a small toy racetrack. The track is equipped with a ramp where you can place a small car, like one of the old Matchbox type race cars.

If you place a car on the ramp, and lift up on the top edge, it triggers the sound of an automobile engine revving up as the car rolls down the ramp.

The Race Track

The toy continues to make this sound until the ramp descends back to the original starting point, then shuts off. To repeat the sound of the car engine, you must lift on the edge of the ramp again.

As Adam and Jessica listened to the sound of the car engine revving up, then shutting off, then revving up again, over and over. They figured that the girls were out of bed playing with the toy.

When Adam got out of bed to see who was up and to put the child back to bed, the noise stopped.

He immediately went to the girl's room to scold whoever had been out of bed but found both girls sleeping.

When Adam returned to bed and told Jessica what had happened, neither had an explanation how the toy turned on and off by itself. Because it is impossible for the sound to be made, without lifting on the ramp.

"The toy can't make the sound without someone manipulating it," Adam explained. *"It's just not possible!"*

This was the one and only time that the toy garage operated on its own.

If it was not one of the Stock's children playing with it, then who was it? Donald, perhaps?

The Doll

The second incident with a toy occurred in the summer of 2018, while Corinna was playing with her Taylor Swift singing fashion doll in her playroom.

If you are not familiar with the doll, it looks similar to a Barbie doll, but has an added feature. If you press on her stomach, it sings a song. Then after a few moments, the doll stops singing, and to continue the song, the child must once again press on the dolls stomach.

"I was in the living room at the time and Corinna was in her playroom playing with the doll. She had been playing for some time, so I thought everything was ok," Adam said.

"Then, out of the blue, she came out of the playroom, and approached me, extending her arms and handed the doll to me. She appeared upset about something, so I asked her what was wrong, to which she replied!

"Daddy, the doll is freaking me out, I don't want to play with it anymore."

"When I asked her why it was freaking her out," Adam continued. *"She told me that as she was playing, she sat the doll on her play desk for a moment. But after doing so, she got the feeling that someone was standing next to her, but she did not see anyone. No sooner than she had the feeling, the floor squeaked several times as if someone were moving about. If that was not enough to frighten her, the doll sang on its own, which isn't possible. When she gave me the doll, I put it on a desk near the kitchen and left it there for the night."*

Corinna's Doll

If the story ended there, it would be creepy enough. But at 142 East Beardstown Street, you learn to expect the unexpected.

The next morning, Jessica had her own experience with the doll.

"It was around 10:00 A.M. the next morning." She explained. *"Adam was at work, and the girls were not at home. I had been downstairs in the restaurant and came upstairs using the elevator to take the towels out of the washer and put them in the clothes dryer. When I stepped off the elevator, I heard the doll singing. The song played over and over. It was freaky!"* Jessica said.

"The doll playing over and over, made little sense, because it is push button activated. Someone has to keep pushing the button over and over for it to keep looping. But it played over and over four times by itself. I didn't know what to do so, I picked it up and moved it and it stopped."

Jessica explained that the doll didn't finish the song like it did when the kids played with it. *"They always hold the button down and let the song play, which drives me crazy,"* She said with a smile. *"But this was different, the song would play, then it would start over. But it never finished the song."*

Since the incidents of the summer of 2018, the doll has never played on its own again.

The Wand

In July of that same year, I was in the building for my third investigation and had a reporter and camera person from WICS TV Channel 20, accompany me for the first couple of hours of the investigation. It was during this time that I had my encounter with a toy turning on by itself.

All the lights were off in the building and I was giving a brief tour to the crew, pointing out where activity takes place.

After giving a tour of the children's playroom, we proceeded to a room adjacent to the playroom at the far south end of the building. I had never experienced or recorded anything in the room, so we didn't spend much time in there before returning to the playroom.

When we did, the camera man noticed a bright blue glowing light coming from the south side of the playroom. At first, we couldn't find the source of the light. Then we noticed that it was coming from a nearby toy-box.

When I checked it out, I found a toy princess magic play wand. The shaft of the wand was clear and had what appeared to be a clear liquid in it with bubbles. At first, I couldn't figure out how to turn it off, but discovered that to turn the light on or off, one must twist the handle.

When I did, it turned off.

It puzzled me how the toy turned on by itself, because shifting or falling over in the toy box would not cause the handle to twist, which is the only way to turn the light on.

I tested my reasoning by sitting the wand in an upright position and knocked it over against other toys several times and nothing happened.

When I told Adam and Jessica about the incident, they said that the wand had never turned on by itself before, nor has it done so since.

Ghost Dog

Scholars have discussed the words soul and spirit at length for many years.

Religious scholars, philosophers and even scientist have offered remarks and theories about the spirit and the soul. But most often, the terms end up meaning the same thing.

But is there a difference?

To find the answer to the question, one must look beyond what philosophers and scientists say and go to the source and asked, *"What does the Bible say about spirits and souls?"*

1 Thessalonians 5:23 says, *"And the God of peace Himself sanctify you wholly and may your **spirit** and **soul** and **body** be preserved complete, without blame, at the coming of our Lord Jesus Christ."*

What this verse tells us is that we are spirit, body and soul. Three unique but connected aspects of life.

This philosophical discussion is of great importance to my next question. *Since animals have a body, do they also have a spirit and soul?*

If so, does their spirit and soul live on after death, existing in the physical world as ghosts, haunting the corridors and grounds they once roamed?

My upbringing taught me that animals don't have spirits or souls.

But now after nineteen years of paranormal investigations, I'm not so sure that what I was led to believe, is true.

Animals experience many of the same emotions as humans do, such as love, anxiety, pain, fear, anger and can reason and figure things out on their own.

Anyone who has been fortunate enough to have the companionship of a loyal dog or cat, can attest that they seem to have their own unique personality.

I have heard about animal hauntings for years, but never experienced the phenomena for myself, never experienced it that is, until I investigated Dr. Ugs and captured what I believe is evidence of a ghost dog, haunting the building, not once, but during two of my investigations.

It wasn't until after I reviewed recorded audio evidence from my Halloween night investigation of 2017, that I found I had recorded the sound of a barking dog.

Not only did I record barking, the sound echoes and sounded like the barking was coming from inside the building and I can assure you, there were no stray dogs in the building that night.

My ten plus years as a private investigator along with an additional nineteen years of experience as a paranormal investigator, has taught me to keep the environment that I investigate as controlled as possible.

Doing so, lessens the chance of mistaking ordinary sounds of the environment for paranormal evidence.

One way that I do this is anytime that I hear a noise, voice or sound of someone or something that comes from outside, I announce what I hear for the recorders.

I didn't hear a dog barking on either of the nights I recorded them during the Dr. Ugs investigations. Because I would have noted this for the recorder.

The barking was loud, so I should have heard it while in the building, but I didn't.

I am certain that the barking came from inside the building, not only because of the volume and intensity of the barking, but because it echoes.

Let me further explain why I am certain that the barking came from within the building.

On the night of October 31, 2017, I set up audio and video recording devices throughout the location as I do on all investigations.

Since I only recorded the barking on audio devices, I will limit my explanation of equipment locations to audio recorders.

I placed seven recorders in the building at various spots, hoping to record disembodied voices and sounds.

The following is a breakdown of where the recorders were placed which will give you an idea of how I was able to determine where the barking emanated from.

One recorder was placed in the basement. One downstairs in the restaurant area on a table ten feet from the front door at the north side of the building. One in the children's playroom on the second floor at the far south end of the building. One in Adam and Jessica's bedroom located adjacent and just north of the playroom. One in the upstairs hallway near the shower where the shadow man wanders about on the east side of the building. One in the children's bedroom just north of Adam and Jessica's bedroom and one in the upstairs kitchen area, on an island, at the far north end of the building.

A quick note: The kitchen and living rooms are next to each other in an open floor plan, with the living room at the far north end of the building.

The kitchen island location is of importance, which you will understand as I further explain.

I recorded the barking dog on four of the seven recorders, which helped to triangulate the proximity of where the barking may have emanated from.

The rooms where the barking was recorded were the playroom, Adam and Jessica's bedroom, the downstairs restaurant area and the recorder on the kitchen island.

I first discovered the barking while reviewing the recorder from the kid's playroom. It was loud and caught me off guard, because I had not heard a dog barking during the investigation.

I was even more perplexed, because not only was the barking loud, it echoed. The dog barks four times in succession, *"ruff, ruff, ruff, ruff!"*

In the background, you can hear the faint rumbling from the engine of a car as it passes by the north side of the building. It sounds as though a dog is chasing a car or running to the window to bark at the car as it passes by.

Trying to explain it, I rationalized that even though it was loud and echoed, the barking must have come from somewhere behind the building.

Since I investigate alone and use multiple recording devices on investigations, it can take me upwards of a month or more to review all the recorded data.

For example, if I use seven audio recorders and three video cameras and am at a location for eight hours, I have eighty hours of data to review. So, it takes time.

For this reason, I like to keep the client informed of the progress of my evidence review and contact them to provide updates, which I did during the Dr. Ugs investigations.

When I contacted Adam to give him an update, I told him about the barking dog and how it sounded like it was coming from inside the building.

Little did I expect Adam's reaction or what he was about to tell me, because he mentioned nothing about a dog during the initial interview with the Stock's.

"That's funny that you say that, Larry!" Adam exclaimed. *Because, several times since we've lived in the building, Jessica has told me that something has awakened her in the middle of the night, that feels like a dog jumping into bed with her.*

"What do you mean?" I questioned.

"Well," Adam continued. *"Jessica told me, she has felt something big, jumping into bed with her. She can feel the bed moving after whatever it is jumps on the bed and experiences what feels like an animal going around in circles, like it is making a comfortable place to lie down. When it stops going in circles, she feels the weight of something big leaning against her."*

Later, when I talked to Jessica, she confirmed what Adam told me. I asked her if she noticed what time of night it is when this happens, and she said that it always occurs a few minutes before midnight.

This would fit the timeframe of my recordings, because all four recorders captured the sound of the dog barking at 11:53 P.M., or seven minutes until midnight!

At the time I gave Adam the update, I had only reviewed recorders from the basement and the children's playroom, and the barking wasn't recorded in the basement. So, it wouldn't be until after reviewing additional recorders that I would find further evidence of a ghost dog.

The next recorder I reviewed was the one from Adam and Jessica's bedroom, located only twenty feet from the recorder in the playroom.

With the close proximity of the recorders, I expected to record the barking in their bedroom as well and I did, also at 11:53 P.M.

I expected the barking on this recorder to be more subdued, because if my assumption that the sound of the barking dog was coming from the south and behind the building was correct. With the recorder in the bedroom located twenty feet further to the north, the sound should be more obscure.

However, to my surprise, it wasn't. Because the barking recorded in the bedroom was even louder and had more of an echo to it than the first recording. This meant that the barking could not have come from behind the building.

"It has to be coming from somewhere in front of the building." I thought to myself. So, since I now believed that there must have been a dog barking in front of the building, I reviewed the audio from the downstairs recorder near the front door.

But as the old saying goes, *"One should never assume."*

As I listened to the audio and watched the time stamp getting closer and closer to 11:53 P.M. on the timeline of my editing software, I expected the sound waves would be off the chart, but they were not.

The barking dog is audible; but, two of the four barks are so subdued, they are hard to hear. Instead of hearing the loud and clear, *"ruff, ruff, ruff, ruff,"* recorded by the first two recorders, *I* could only hear a faint, *"ruff, ruff,"* unless I boosted the volume of the audio clip.

So, what did this mean?

It meant that if the barking didn't come from in front of the building at street level and the sound of the barking was louder in Adam and Jessica's bedroom, than in the playroom, it had to be coming from upstairs, somewhere at the center of the Stocks residence, and from inside the building.

The one consistent piece of evidence from the downstairs recorder was that I recorded it at 11:53 P.M.

I next reviewed audio from the recorders in the upstairs hallway and the recorder in the kid's bedroom. Both recorders were within twenty-five feet of the recorder in Adam and Jessica's bedroom, where so far, the barking had been the loudest.

With the proximity of the recorders to the Stocks bedroom, I was sure that they would also record the barking, helping to further triangulate where it was coming from, but neither of the recorders picked up the barking.

This made little sense, because all the recorders I use are identical Sony recorders, capable of picking up sound from several hundred feet away.

Many times, over the years, I have had this same experience with recorded EVP.

There have been investigations I have had multiple recorders located close to each other, and only one or two will pick up sounds while others don't.

Sometimes, I hear nothing at all. But when I review the audio, I find I recorded things I didn't hear. Other times, I hear voices and noises, and when I review the recording, nothing is there.

Recorders, not picking up the barking in the same proximity of recorders that did, leads me to believe that what I recorded are legitimate EVP's and are recordings of a dog haunting the building.

The last recorder I reviewed was the one I had placed in the kitchen.

So far, the barking was loudest in Adam and Jessica's bedroom, and because it was almost in-audible downstairs, I concluded that it must come from near their bedroom.

But, as I have learned, one must expect the unexpected when dealing with the paranormal. Because when I listened to the audio from the kitchen, I could not believe what I heard.

Not only had I recorded the barking on the recorder in the kitchen, the volume of the barking was louder than recorded by any other recorders.

It was so loud that I am certain the barking dog emanated from the kitchen area. Not only was it loud and echoed, it was resounding.

When I presented the evidence from the October investigation, it convinced Adam and Jessica that a dog was inside the building the night of my investigation.

"I have heard dogs barking at night since living in the building." Adam Said. *"But they sounded nothing like what you recorded! The barking we hear is faint and we can tell it comes from the outside. This is different."*

Hayden

During the October evidence presentation, the Stocks shared information with me about the previous owners, that they had not shared prior to my investigation and which may relate to the phantom dog.

When Mike and Susan Carson owned Dr. Ugs, they too lived above the business, but they did not live alone, as they shared their home with their beloved, Wheaten terrier dog, Hayden.

Each morning, Mike would take Hayden across the street to the courtyard, so that Hayden could take care of business.

One morning as Mike was cleaning up after Hayden, their treasured dog ran across the street, headed back to the restaurant, and was hit and killed by a passing car.

In late summer of 2018, the Stocks invited me to meet Mike and Susan, so I could play the recordings of the phantom dog for them, to see if what I recorded sounded like Hayden.

It can be awkward the first time that you meet someone to present paranormal evidence. But the Carson's were told in advance what I do and the reason that I was coming, so there were no surprises.

Right from the start, I could tell that Susan was more receptive of spirits and hauntings than Mike. Not that Mike does not believe that such things are possible, but he is more of the *"I have to see it to believe it,"* school of thought, when it comes to ghost and haunted places, which is understandable.

When I finished playing the four recordings of the barking dog, Susan spoke up first. She agreed that yes, to her, the recordings sounded like Hayden's bark. Mike agreed that it was a dog and that it sounded like it was coming from inside the building but was not sure if it sounded like Hayden or not.

Jessica told her story to the Carson's of being awakened from a sound sleep, by what feels like a dog jumping into bed with her and making itself comfortable.

I asked the Carson's if they let Hayden on the bed when they lived in the building and although the answer was no, Susan explained the following.

"When we would leave to go somewhere, sometimes we left Hayden at home free to roam the upstairs. Most often, when we returned home, we would find the bedspread disarranged as if he had sprawled out on the bed." She said with a smile.

"There is something else that I should tell you that may relate to what's taking place." Susan continued.

"After Hayden's death, Mike and I would hear his dog tags rattling and jingling as if he were still running around the building. Not only did we hear it in the building, but we heard it coming from the back seat of our car."

"*I might be a skeptic,*" Mike said. "*But I heard it too. I can't explain it, but I heard it. It was the darndest thing!*"

On April 17, 2019, I investigated the building for the fifth time and once again recorded the sound of a barking dog. The barking from the 2019 investigation was louder than the EVP from the kitchen on Halloween night, 2017.

Even more interesting. After the dog barks, there is a gruff man's voice, that sounds like he is scolding the dog to be quiet. Following the voice, the dog barks a second time. I recorded the EVP sequence at 4:49 A.M. in the children's playroom.

Similar to what happened during the October 2017 investigation, I had multiple recorders placed near each other and only one recorder captured the sound of the dog and voice of the man. Which makes no sense.

When you add up the evidence, which includes EVPs, Jessica experiencing something jumping into bed with her on multiple occasions and the Carson's hearing what sounded like Hayden's dog tags jingling after his death. One could conclude that a dog, maybe Hayden, haunts the former funeral home at 142 East Beardstown Street.

The Woman's Voice

On December 17, 2018, while babysitting the girls, Adam had an experience that he won't soon forget.

Jessica was out shopping and Adam; Corinna and Ella were upstairs in the kitchen area. At one point, Ella, who was carrying her blanket, started walking toward the kitchen door that leads to the main hallway.

As she was exiting the room, Adam heard a voice. It was a woman's voice and sounded like she said something to Ella. Thinking he was imagining things and must have mistook Ella's voice for that of an older woman, he turned to walk away, but noticed the puzzled look on Corinna's face.

"Daddy!" Corinna said. *"Did mommy come home?"*

"No, why sweetie?" Adam questioned.

"If mommy's not home, who was the lady that was talking?"

"When Corinna asked me who the lady was that was talking, a cold chill ran down my spine! Because I knew it wasn't my imagination, she heard the voice too."

"When Corinna and I heard the woman's voice, Ella was about the same age that Corinna was when we heard her talking to her invisible friend Donald," Adam explained.

"In the back of my mind, I always wondered, that if this place has ghosts, would Ella also be able to see and talk to them like Corinna did, when she got to be the age Corinna was?"

The Boy in the Bathroom

In September 2018, I was at work and was conversing with two friends, Mark Taylor and Scott McCullar.

I was telling them about my investigation at Dr. Ugs and the evidence that I obtained. As I was explaining some things that have taken place, Scott interrupted and stopped me.

"Wait a minute," He said. *"I know the place you are talking about, because I had something weird happen to me there."*

"January 2, 2017, I attended a wedding reception at Dr. Ugs." He continued.

"During the evening, I needed to use the bathroom, so I walked toward the back of the building, past the bar where the bathrooms are. The doors to both the men's and women's bathrooms were closed. So, I reached for the door handle of the men's bathroom to open it. When I did, I heard giggling and the voices of what sounded like children inside the bathroom."

"Figuring that they were horsing around but got the message that someone needed to use the bathroom when I jiggled the doorknob, I waited." Scott said.

"But, after several minutes, they didn't come out. I was getting a little perturbed and tired of waiting, so I knocked on the door and all became quiet. I pulled on the door handle thinking they locked it, but it opened. When I looked in the room, to my surprise, it was empty."

Puzzled by what had happened, after using the bathroom and washing his hands, Scott returned to the reception.

He knew the priest who performed the ceremony, so he went over to talk to him and mentioned what had happened.

"Scott, my friend," said the priest. *"Look around and tell me what you see?"*

"When I looked around, I knew what he was referring to," Scott said. *"I noticed that there weren't any children in attendance. Because it was an all adult affair."*

Doors closing and locking on their own

In July 2018, I investigated the building for the third time. Of the five investigations conducted at Dr. Ugs, I only had three personal experiences that I would consider out of the ordinary. One such event took place during the July investigation.

It was a little past 1:00 A.M. and I headed downstairs to hang out in the bar area for a while.

As I exited out the door leading to the stairwell, I left the door ajar to make sure it didn't accidently lock on me.

I have done this ever since an incident took place during an investigation at the Morrison House on the grounds of the Christian County Historical Society in Taylorville.

The incident at the Morrison House was bizarre and involved a door, locking on its own.

An investigator named Jay accompanied me on the investigation. We had access to all the buildings on the grounds, including the Pence Building, which houses the main business offices and the bathroom.

We had taken several bathroom breaks during the night and each time that we did; we left the Morrison House unlocked to make for easy access upon returning to investigate.

It was 2:30 A.M. and we were returning from one of our breaks. As we approached the house, I reached for the doorknob on the front door. I made the comment to Jay. *"Wouldn't it suck if the door was locked."*

No sooner than I said this, I reached for the doorknob and heard a clicking sound. When I tried to open the door, I couldn't, because it had locked.

Making it even more perplexing. The lock was a non-deadlocking style of lock, meaning it does not lock by itself. Luckily, I had grabbed the key from the kitchen table before we headed for our break, so we were able to get back in.

For the next twenty minutes, we slammed, re-slammed and pulled the door shut, over and over and could not get it to lock on its own.

The lock on the door to the loft at Dr. Ugs is like the lock on the door at the Morrison house.

Even though I knew it should not lock on its own, I left the door ajar when I headed downstairs.

When I returned a half hour later, it surprised me to find that the door was closed, as if someone had pulled it shut.

A simple draft would not create enough airflow to close the door tight, as it takes physical force to do so.

Luckily, the door did not lock, so I was able to get back into the Stocks residence.

I didn't think much about the incident, until the following Saturday, when I sent a text message to Adam, to give him an update of my evidence review.

During our text exchange, I received the following message from Adam.

"Tonight, I am home alone and have had a creepy feeling all night, like something is off about the place. Earlier, when Jessica and the kids left, I went downstairs with them to see them off. I was the last one to leave and didn't lock the door because I was coming right back." He explained.

"When I came back upstairs, the door was locked, and I couldn't get in. But to lock the door, you have to push a button down from inside. So, the door can only lock from inside the apartment. You can't use a key from the outside to lock or unlock the door." Adam further explained.

"Thank God the elevator was down on the first floor. I rode it up and got in using the back entrance. But since the locking of the door, there has been an uneasy feeling about the place."

Although the door didn't lock on me during the July investigation, the experiences that Adam and I had were similar and as I mentioned in my story about the Morrison House incident. The type of locks on the doors can't lock by themselves. So how they became locked on their own, remains a mystery.

Poltergeist Activity

Doors locking and closing on their own, toys turning on by themselves, and phantom footsteps. These are occurrences often associated with poltergeist activity.

For those of you not familiar with the term, poltergeist. Poltergeist is a German word, that means, noisy ghost.

Some believe they are spirits or supernatural forces that can manipulate objects, move furniture, and yes, even lock and unlock doors.

These types of things have been experienced at Dr. Ugs by the Stock family, their employees, guest and even me.

As I mentioned earlier, my first investigation took place on Halloween night of 2017 and it only took a matter of minutes, before I had my first experience with the strangeness that the building has to offer.

I had only been in the building for forty-five minutes and was downstairs in the bar area, setting up equipment.

Tape recorders and video cameras were already in place and recording upstairs. As I was putting new batteries in one of my recorders, out of nowhere I heard a loud ruckus from upstairs.

It sounded like someone was dragging a piece of furniture across the wood floor and the noise was loud.

I grabbed a flashlight and ran to the staircase and headed upstairs.

When I entered the door to the residence, it was quiet. I combed the entire upstairs from one end to the other, looking for the origin of the noise, but saw nothing that looked like it had moved and there were no signs of scratches or damage to the wood floor.

I rewound my video cameras and reviewed the footage, but they recorded nothing unusual.

"Surely my audio recorders captured the racket." I thought to myself. But when I checked them, nothing had been recorded on audio either.

Over the years, I have heard loud crashes and the sound of slamming doors that were so loud they startled me, only to review audio and video equipment and find that the equipment didn't record the sounds. This is part of the frustration that comes with investigating the paranormal.

More and more, I believe the supernatural only allows us to record what they want us to.

As if they are not concerned if we keep searching, but do not want us to or are not allowed to let us capture clear-cut evidence of their existence in our realm.

I am not the only one who has heard furniture being dragged and moved about, as Jessica's mother, and several of the staff working in the restaurant have also witnessed these things.

Soon after the Stocks moved into the building, Jessica's mother heard furniture being moved and dragged about when no one else was around. As with my experience, she found nothing out of place.

Two former waitresses told me stories of witnessing utensils slide off tables and chairs scoot across the floor, when no one was near them.

Jessica hears music playing but so far cannot detect where it is coming from or determine the time period of the music.

These types of experiences are what makes the paranormal so fascinating and at times makes it difficult to relax in your own home.

The Man in the Mirror

*When you get what you want in your struggle for self
and the world makes you king for a day.
Just go to the mirror and look at yourself
and see what that man has to say.*

*For it isn't your father, or mother, or wife
whose judgment upon you must pass.
The fellow whose verdict counts most in your life
is the one staring back from the glass.
He's the fellow to please — never mind all the rest
for he's with you, clear to the end.
And you've passed your most difficult, dangerous test
if the man in the glass is your friend.*

You may fool the whole world down the pathway of years

and get pats on the back as you pass.
But your final reward will be heartache and tears
if you've cheated the man in the glass.

– Dale Wimbrow, 1934

When I first read Dale Wimbrow's poem, *The Man in the Mirror*, I thought of a story Jessica told me of her own encounters with a man in a mirror.

"I have seen him several times." Jessica said. *"It's always when I am downstairs working at the kitchen sink, that I glimpse something out of the corner of my eye. When I turn and look, I see the reflection of a man in the mirror, standing at the south end of the bar, closest to the kitchen. He looks like a real person. But when I leave the kitchen to see who is there, I find no one."*

Jessica explained that she sees him midafternoon and has seen him several times.

When I asked what the man looks like, she said that he is a bigger man with light-colored hair. She is not sure why, but she gets the feeling that he is non-threatening.

After reading Wimbrow's poem, I wondered if the reason the man still hangs around is the same as the axiom of the poem. Which is. *"One never finds peace or happiness, unless we approve of what we see, when we look in the mirror."*

So, is the phantom man still earthbound because he is ashamed of something that he did or didn't do while living, and too afraid to move on to face judgement?

Or is he still here facing judgement of the strongest kind. His own self-imposed judgement?

Investigator's Personal Experience

Obtaining evidence of paranormal activity comes from two sources. Credible eyewitness accounts and recorded evidence in the form of audio, video and photos.

You have already read about the myriad of eyewitness accounts as told to me by the Stocks, their employees and my friend, Scott McCullar.

Based on the decade of training and experience that I had as a private investigator which encompassed interviewing thousands of people from all walks of life. I believe that the Stocks, and the other witnesses that I interviewed during my investigation, are credible.

Besides their stories, I too witnessed things that I couldn't explain, including hearing furniture being dragged across the floor, seeing a child's toy lighting up on its own, and finding a door I had left ajar, closed and latched.

But one incident that took place during my final investigation the night of April 17, 2019, stands out above all the others and helped confirm for me, something haunts the building. It is an event that sends a cold chill down my spine whenever I think about it.

The time was five minutes until three o'clock in the morning or, as some prefer to call it, the bewitching hour. I was in Adam and Jessica's bedroom, sitting at the foot of their bed, on a loveseat.

From my vantage point, I could see the video camera I had mounted on a tripod and placed in between the half wall that separates the Stocks bedroom from the kids' bedroom.

The reason I could see the camera and tripod in the obscure lighting, was because of light coming from the courtyard across the street, that was shining through a window transom, above the doorway leading to the hall.

I used the love seat as my primary observation point, since it allowed me to monitor much of the upstairs from there.

At one point, as I was gazing toward the camera, without warning, I heard what sounded like a deep breath, as if someone had exhaled.

The sound came from behind me and to my right.

The hair stood up on the back of my neck. Goosebumps popped up on my arms and legs and a cold chill went down my back.

Not knowing who or what had made the sound or what I might see, I turned my head, while switching on my flashlight.

Scanning the room, the beam from the light reflected off a mirror atop a vanity, blinding me.

As I continued turning my head, the light from my flashlight lit up the area in the direction the breath had come from.

I saw nothing unusual, but now felt that I was being watched from the shadows by someone or something.

Upstairs Floorplan

Convinced that I was not imagining what I heard, I remained seated and turned off the flashlight.

I hoped that who, or whatever made the sound, would do it again. Well, as they say, be careful what you wish for, lest it come true.

Several minutes passed, and I was at the point where I was wondering if maybe I imagined what I thought I heard.

I again felt static electricity on the back of my neck, causing the hair to stand up like it had done a few minutes earlier.

No sooner than this happened, I heard the sound again. It was the same breathy exhaling.

It was a deep breath and sounded like it was only a few feet away. I knew that it was not the sound of the air conditioner or equipment from the restaurant, because Adam had turned everything off before leaving.

I froze and listened for movement, but there was not any.

Again, turning on my flashlight, I looked to my right and could see the wall behind me.

There was nothing there.

Remaining still I rotated my head in the opposite direction, back toward the left, still scanning the room with the flashlight.

When I looked toward the video camera attached to the tripod, I could not see the video camera, nor could I see the light coming from the courtyard across the street that had been shining through the window transom.

At first, I was not sure what was going on, then I saw it.

Standing a few feet from me and blocking my line of sight toward the video camera, was a solid, black silhouette of what looked like a short person. It was the size and shape of a child only three or four feet tall.

The figure was so dark that it blocked out the video camera for several seconds, then lunged forward and vanished.

"What the hell?" I said to myself.

What I saw was the silhouette of a person, although a small one; there one minute and gone the next, vanishing into the darkness.

As soon as it disappeared, I could once again see the video camera perched atop the tripod. When the phantom shadow lunged forward, it was facing toward the children's room, so I jumped up and headed into their room.

I shined my flashlight from floor to ceiling looking for the illusive figure but saw nothing.

For the next twenty minutes, I tried to recreate and demystify what I saw.

To replicate what I had been doing just prior to seeing the figure, I turned my head to my right and stared into the dark obscure shadows, then turned back and looked toward the camera, to see if this caused my eyes to play tricks on me and in effect, block out the video camera.

But try as I may, I could not recreate what took place. Because each time that I would turn back and look toward the camera, it was visible, as was the light shining through the transom.

"Did I just see the shadowy image of Corinna's invisible friend Donald or some other ghostly visitor?" I thought to myself.

I am not sure if I saw Donald or not, but I saw something. Something that I cannot explain and something that I could not recreate using the same circumstances.

Then I remembered what Adam had told me just a few days before the investigation. He talked of seeing small shadowy movements out of the corner of his eyes, as if something were there in his peripheral. But when he looked, whatever he saw was gone. He told me that what he was seeing was the approximate size of a child.

What I saw was like what Adam described in the days leading up to my investigation. But unlike Adam, I did not see it out of the corner of my eyes. Because it was right in front of me before it moved and vanish.

As you will read in the *EVP Evidence Summary*, besides seeing the small shadowy figure, I also recorded several EVP's of voices of children. The EVP's add additional proof to help validate the eyewitness accounts that the building is occupied by at least one ghost child and maybe more.

EVP Evidence

Beyond seeing ghostly entities, which I have seen seven in the nineteen years that I have been investigating the paranormal. The factor above all else that keeps me coming back for more, are the unexplained voices and sounds that I have recorded over the years.

Not only has audio evidence kept me coming back for more, it has convinced me, that ghost, supernatural beings, creatures from other realms or whatever these unexplained visitors are, can somehow access our world to roam about.

I have recorded hundreds of EVPs, with the quality ranging from impossible to understand, to distinct and indisputable in what is being said.

No location, however, has yielded the number or clarity of EVPs as Dr. Ugs has. So why is this?

Is it because the building once housed a funeral home? Or is there something about the land where the building sits, that allows spirits to come and go as they please, like a supernatural portal or energy vortex?

Does the activity relate to Jessica's sensitivity to spirits? Or is it a combination of all the above?

To tell you I know the answer to the question would be dishonest. Because I don't know.

I hope that future investigations at Dr. Ugs will reveal new evidence in the form of EVPs and personal experiences, allowing me to explain at least some of what goes on.

For me, the most puzzling aspect of my five investigations at Dr. Ugs, is the lack of personal experiences I had. One would think, with all the recorded evidence, I would have heard and experienced much more than I did.

It was like there was a paranormal extravaganza going on right under my nose, that I was oblivious to.

But, anyone who has investigated or experienced the paranormal as often as I have, knows that there is no rhyme or reason in the way paranormal activity unfolds, and just when you think you have one of its mysteries figured out, new factors arise and the equation changes.

Since there were, so many EVPs recorded, I will limit my evidence analysis to the best of the best, beginning with my first investigation.

EVPs from the October 31, 2017 Investigation

11:53 P.M. (Multiple locations)

I recorded five different EVPs that were distinct during the October investigation.

One of the EVPs, the barking dog, was discussed earlier in the book and was recorded by four different audio recorders at 11:53 P.M. So, I will not go into detail to its significance in this evidence summary, but I believe it is evidence of a ghost dog.

In the earlier discussion, I explained why I believe the barking originated from within the building, upstairs, near the adjoining kitchen and living room areas.

The barking dog was the first piece of evidence that I recorded during the October 31 investigation. Like the other EVP's that I have recorded at Dr. Ugs, I didn't hear the barking when it was recorded.

I recorded the EVP in the playroom, Adam and Jessica's bedroom, the adjoining kitchen and living room and downstairs in the restaurant near the front door.

11:59 P.M. (Kitchen)

Because of the story that Adam and Jessica told me of the kid's toy race track, playing on its own in the middle of the night, I tried to coax a response out of the phantom guilty of playing with the toy and waking the couple from a sound sleep.

To do so, I conducted an EVP session, asking questions aloud, trying to invoke a response from a spirit, with the purpose of hearing the response real-time, recording it or in a best-case scenario, both.

Although I am basing my assumption on speculation, the possibility that Corinna's invisible friend Donald, may be the spirit guilty of playing with the kid's toys, is high. I can't prove this, but it makes sense.

I asked several questions during the EVP session without a reply, or so I thought. Because when I examined my recorders, I found a response to something I said.

My statement was: *"I don't know how to make the racetrack work. Let me know how it works!"*

The feedback that I recorded was, *"I won't!"*

I was standing near the convergence of the playroom and Adam and Jessica's bedroom when the verbal exchange took place

The response was faint, but when I enhanced the volume using editing software, I could hear and understand it.

Not hearing the response but recording it was perplexing. Much like what happened during the April 2019 investigation.

If you will recall, I had many recorders set up near each other and only one captured the barking dog and voice of a man.

Once again, I had various recorders set up, four of which picked up my voice asking the question. But only the recording device in the kitchen, the one furthest from where I asked the question, captured the *"I won't"* response.

12:46 A.M. (Playroom)

The next EVP leads me to believe that spirits are aware of what we are doing. I was taking a bathroom break and was in the upstairs bathroom.

This was the first time that I had been in the bathroom and was looking for the light switch when I bumped the wall with my elbow making a slight sound.

I did not hear the voice when it spoke, but when I checked my audio recorder in the toy room, it was there.

The voice says, *"Hit Wall!"* As has been the circumstance with several EVPs I have recorded at Dr. Ugs. There were other recorders closer to the bathroom than the one in the playroom, but none of them captured what was said.

2:20 A.M. (Basement)

I have talked little about the basement, but the bowels of an old funeral home can be downright frightening and cause you to look over your shoulder as you wander in the dark. Especially when you wander alone as I do.

Even the trip to the basement is hair-raising, as the only way to get to the understructure of the building is by taking an old platform style elevator. A design reminiscent of something you might expect to find in medieval times.

It squeaks and squeals as it lowers its passengers, drowning out any sounds of the surroundings until you reach your destination.

Then, as the platform descends below the top of the doorframe to the basement, the only thing you see is darkness and you feel you are being watched as you continue your descent.

I remember shining my flashlight, half expecting someone or something to be standing in await of my arrival.

Neither Adam nor Jessica are fond of going to the basement, and both have said as much.

When the time comes to swap out empty soda canisters for the restaurant, they draw straws to decide who the unlucky one is that must make the dreadful trip to the basement to change the canister.

Part of their uneasiness when going to the basement is knowing that the building was at one time a funeral home.

I'm sure that most would not relish the thought of going to the dark cellar by themselves.

On the other hand, their daughter Corinna doesn't seem bothered by the basement which makes me wonder, if at some point, she encountered her phantom friend Donald down there and isn't afraid.

To take it a step further. If Donald was a child playmate to Corinna, maybe her mind was more on having fun with him, than worrying about the darkness and what else may be in the shadows of the underground catacomb.

Plus, she was always accompanied by one of her parents when in the basement. With children, there is no safer feeling than when mom or dad is at your side.

When you get to the July 3, 2018 EVP summary, you will read about a chilling EVP that I recorded in the basement of a child's voice.

View from the Elevator

But before we jump too far ahead, I'll discuss a voice I recorded in the basement during the October 2017 investigation.

The basement runs from the elevator on the south end of the building to the sidewalk in front of Dr. Ugs to the north, where an old coal shoot and coal storage room sits underneath the sidewalk.

One of the more unnerving aspects of investigating the basement and not even taking into consideration that the building is a former funeral home, is the isolation and seclusion from the outside world, when you are down there alone.

Plus, if you run into the phantoms that haunt the building while in the basement. There is only one way out and more than likely, you will have to pass by who or whatever is there, to get to the elevator for a very slow trip to safety.

As I investigated the basement, the only sounds I heard were the occasional sound of the furnace kicking on and dripping water coming from the street and seeping down the old coal shoot.

Not until after I reviewed audio from a recorder I had placed on an old table in the central part of the basement; did I realize I had recorded a voice at 2:20 A.M.

The voice is male and says *"Hey!"*

It sounded gruff but is clear. It was as though it was trying to get someone's attention and since I was the only person in the basement, or maybe I should say, living person, I assume that the voice is talking to me.

This would be the only EVP recorded in the basement on this night.

5:17 A.M.
The 5:17 A.M. EVP is one of the more fascinating and thought-provoking EVPs that I have recorded since becoming a paranormal investigator and is one that I mentioned earlier, while discussing the James Potter shooting.

I believe this EVP is of great importance because of a possible connection to the 1929 shooting incident.

Looking back, it seems like something wanted the sequence recorded.

Standard procedure for me is to wrap up investigations by 5:00 A.M., but for this investigation, I stayed longer and did not finish until after 5:30 A.M.

A recorder in the children's bedroom was the only recorder to capture the EVP, even though other recorders were nearby.

When it was recorded, I was sitting on the loveseat at the foot of the Stocks bed. Moments before the EVP, you can hear me move to adjust the position I am sitting for better comfort.

Following the movement, I recorded a loud and distinct bang that sounds like a gunshot.

Two and a half seconds after the gunshot, is a brusque sounding male voice that says, *"Shot Him!"*

There is no mistaking what the voice says, because it is crystal clear. The odds of recording the gunshot sound, followed by a voice saying, shot him, and the two not relate to each other, would be astronomical.

When weighing the evidence, one must decide if we can connect the gunshot and voice to the building, which seems plausible.

If we can, the question becomes twofold.

Who is the person talking and who did they shoot?

Based on the history of the building, the logical conclusion is the voice was either Charles Davis, the service station attendant, reliving shooting James Potter or guilt ridden Alfred Dodd's, the junior partner of the Virgin and Dodd's Funeral home who told the two men to, *"Get outside if you want to settle your differences."*

If we can connect the EVP to the building, then can we also connect the shadowy figure of the man who roams the upstairs hallway to the shooting?

Could the figure be Charles Davis, the shooter, James Potter the victim or Alfred Dodd's, reliving the tragic event. To take this point further, do all three roam the hallway?

Jessica told me during my interview with her, the shadowy figure she has seen on two occasions, didn't appear to be aware she was nearby, but more focused on its own personal mission, whatever that may be.

One theory I have may explain one of the least understood and counter factual aspects of hauntings, the residual haunting.

A residual haunting is a subject that has been debated for decades and an occurrence that may take place in the upstairs hallway of Dr. Ugs.

The consensus among paranormal investigators I have talked to, is the phenomena, is the recording or imprint of a tragic event in the time continuum.

They believe a past event was so tragic the emotional impact of what happened, causes extreme energy which imbeds in the environment.

This results in the event repeating itself in a loop. So, if you are in the right place at the right time or depending on your comfort level for ghostly things. The wrong place at the wrong time, you see the event unfold.

To me, the theory makes little sense. Taking into consideration, the number of tragic events that take place daily, we should witness hundreds if not thousands of these events in our lifetime, which isn't the case.

I base my belief in relation to residual hauntings on the things I have seen since investigating the paranormal and has more of a spiritual or doctrinal basis behind it.

I believe when our time is up in the physical world and we move on to the afterlife, all negativity, calamity and misfortune that we experienced as human beings, stays behind and inherited by the physical world that we once lived.

Our personal problems, worries and unpleasant experiences, remain behind to exists and linger, while we move on to the other side, or Heaven as I prefer to call it, where negative things no longer matter or exist.

So, if my theory is correct, then the gunshot and voice that I recorded could be the lingering earthbound essence of a sorrowful act that Charles Davis committed and re-lives or a guilt-ridden Albert Dodd's reliving a regrettable directive.

If this is the case, is it possible that Adam and Jessica witnessed the reliving of the lingering earthbound guilt, as the shadowy figure?

Once again, as was the case when I recorded the dog barking and the man's voice during the April 17, 2019 investigation. I had multiple recorders set up near the device that recorded the gunshot and voice.

The only recorder, however, that captured the evidence was the one I had placed in the children's bedroom. None of the other nearby recorders, recorded it.

I have had this happen many times over the years, and my only conclusion, although it be speculation, is that some of these paranormal voices and sounds occur in a vortex or portal, that may envelop and insulate the sound from carrying to other nearby recorders.

My theory of vortexes and portals is just one of many attributed to this phenomenon by paranormal investigators.

Hopefully, our theories and guesswork will pay off and lead to proof.

EVPs from the April 2, 2018 Investigation

This investigation yielded the least amount of information of my five investigations at Dr. Ugs and overall was uneventful. But, when you take into consideration that the stocks live there and most days, experience nothing unusual at all, this is not unexpected.

I did however capture two clear EVPs recorded by audio recorders and two voices recorded by an SB-7 device better known as a "spirit box."

I will first discuss the EVPs and before discussing what I heard and recorded using the spirit box, will explain how the device works.

9:56 P.M.

I captured the first EVP of the April 2018 investigation upstairs at 9:56 P.M. I placed the recorder that picked it up on the dresser in the east hallway and was nowhere near the recorder, as I was down in the basement.

The voice is a male voice and says, *"I will say!"* Since I do not understand what it was referring to, I will not bother to speculate. But I can say that several of the male voices recorded in the building sound like they come from the same phantom.

11:57 P.M.

The EVP at 11:57 P.M., was recorded by the same device that recorded the voice at 9:56 P.M. What is interesting about the two voices, is they sound alike. Even more interesting, the 11:57 P.M. EVP, correlates to remodeling done to the upstairs.

The voice says, *"Wall is hidden."*

"Wall is hidden," may relate to a section of wall at the southeast corner of the upstairs living area. I found this out when I played the recorded evidence for Adam and Jessica. The couple told me that at one time, there was another staircase near the elevator shaft and laundry facility upstairs and because of remodeling was closed in. Or as the strange voice said, *"Wall is hidden."*

Was the voice telling me that there is a hidden wall for a reason? If so, what is the importance?

SB-7 Spirit Box

The SB-7 is a mini AM-FM frequency sweeper, which is an altered radio that can be fine-tuned to scan AM or FM radio frequencies, forward or backwards, at a rate measured in milliseconds.

The scan-lock mechanism on the radio is disabled. Therefore, the device continuously scans radio frequencies at a predetermined rate.

Sort of like twisting the knob on a radio backwards and forwards quickly, to produce random noise.

The original device was invented by amateur radio enthusiast Frank Sumption, who read an article about recording EVP that appeared in *Popular Electronics* magazine.

Sumption built a radio receiver he believed allowed real-time communication between the living and the dead and entities from other dimensions.

I chatted many times with Frank on Facebook and we had some interesting conversations to say the least.

He didn't care for paranormal investigators for the most part, but he said he liked me because I didn't believe that most spirits are evil demons. Plus, we were like-minded in that both he and I believe that many of the unexplained things that paranormal investigators encounter is interdimensional rather than spirit.

At first, I didn't buy into the box working. I believed it was nothing more than radio static or skip coming through, along with a phenomenon known as audio pareidolia.

Audio pareidolia is the process of our mind, trying to make sense out of sounds and words and correlate what we hear to familiar words and sounds.

I soon changed my mind, as I noticed how specific information coming through the box were answering questions that I asked.

In addition, at the rate that I scan the frequencies, whole words and complete sentences should not be coming through, when they are being vocalized by the same voice.

One frustrating thing about the box is that on some nights, it is useless and all I get from it is a headache because of the constant white noise. Then, on other nights, the most amazing communication comes through with answers to specific questions about the location.

It takes a lot to convince me that a device like the SB-7 works, but I have heard so many voices coming through with answers to questions I asked, many that are unique to my investigation.

When using the SB-7 box, I always record the sessions, as it seems to be easier to understand what is being said by listing to the recording of the session, than it is hearing the session real time. Plus, when I record what comes through, I have proof of what was said.

I conducted two SB-7 box sessions on April 2. One in the Kitchen and one in the playroom.

The eerie thing when using the box while investigating alone. Is that you can hear the voices coming through, but you cannot hear sound from the surrounding environment due to the intense sound of the white noise coming through the speaker.

With the lights off during investigations, I rely on my sense of hearing to know if anyone or anything is around.

But when the box is in use, you get a sense of vulnerability because you can only hear the noise from the box.

It's the old "fight or flight" feeling where you feel you are being watched or someone is behind you. When this happens, I catch myself glancing over my shoulder, just to make sure no one is there.

9:35 P.M.

The closest audio recorder for the spirit box session in the kitchen was ten feet away, so if a voice came through the box the recorder should capture it.

During one of my conversations with Frank Sumption, he told me that in his experience using the box, his best results were obtained by turning the box on and listening to what they say.

"No need to asked questions Larry, they know who you are and what you will ask."

Much of what Frank said seems true based on my experience with the box. He listened to the box every day, so I'm sure he had data to back his reasoning.

Many times, over the years, just as Frank said, I have heard my name, *"Larry"* said loud and clear as soon as I turn on the device. So, I agree they know who we are.

One point I disagree with Frank on is letting the box run and recording their responses, because this has never worked for me.

When I try this, I get nothing. It's only when I asked a question, that I get activity and verbal responses from the box.

I started the session by asking the standard questions, such as, *"Can you tell me your name? How many spirits are present? Did you either live or die in the building?* Questions of this sort.

The more questions I asked, the more voices came through the box. Most of which were too distorted to understand.

Then a very clear male voice came through that said.

"Hey, get out!"

One interesting aspect of the *"Hey get out,"* voice, is that it was also recorded by a recorder in the playroom but was not picked up by my recorder in Adam and Jessica's bedroom, which was much closer.

The voice didn't sound angry but sounded more matter of fact in tone. Telling me or someone else to get out.

I have talked to other investigators who have recorded similar statements coming through spirit boxes. More times than not, they tell me that, *"A voice came through the box that told me to get out."*

This is one way to take what is said, but I often wonder if some voices could be spirits or interdimensional beings looking out for us and are telling some other imperceptible being that may be present or around us, to get out and not bother us

With no way to prove this theory, it adds another possibility to the mystery of the world of the paranormal.

1:22 A.M.

The second spirit box session began at 1:15 A.M. and took place in the playroom.

I placed the device on the floor and turned the volume to the highest setting. The closest audio recorder was again only ten feet away.

Most of what came through the box was hard to understand. Hard to understand that is, until I asked a specific question related to someone connected to the building.

"Is the man here, who shot James Potter?" I asked.

Seven different sounding voices responded within twenty seconds of my question.

Each of the voices were indistinct, with the exception for two.

Of the voices that I could understand, the first one came through eight and a half seconds after I asked my question. It says, *"Yeah,"* and is female.

The second intelligible voice came four seconds after the woman's voice or twelve and a half seconds after I asked my question.

Not only was the voice's response relevant to my question. It proves that whoever or whatever these voices are, can either hear us through the box, or are close enough in proximity that they can hear us in the flesh.

My belief is that they are nearby, but in a spectrum of light that we cannot see or detect.

The voice that responded was male and says. *"I knew Enzo Potter!"*

Through the research that both the Stock's and I have done on the building and the James Potter shooting. We have found no record of an Enzo Potter or any connection of a person by this name, to James Potter or the building.

I conducted an internet search on the name Enzo Potter. I found a musician who has original music on YouTube and a boy who has his own Facebook page but nothing relevant to my investigation.

Where the name Enzo Potter becomes relevant, is that the voice who heard and responded to my question seems to say. *"No, I don't know of a James Potter, but I knew Enzo Potter."*

Which means he or it, heard the name, Potter.

If this doesn't prove that something out there can hear and communicate with us through the box. Then I'm not sure what will.

So, the question remains, who or what are they?

Are they ghost, spirits, time travelers, interdimensional or some other unknown being or creatures?

No matter who or what they are, I consider the response a major piece of paranormal evidence.

EVPs from the July 3, 2018 Investigation

July 3 was the night that a reporter, *"Leslie Moreno"* and a camera person from News Channel 20 from Springfield, Illinois, accompanied me during the first couple of hours of my investigation.

They were doing a story on the paranormal for their Halloween broadcast later that year.

The night the story was to air, a shooting happened in Springfield and the Halloween segment was never telecast.

The investigation turned out to be fruitful because I recorded ten EVPs and one voice through the *"Spirit Box."*

If you will recall, it was during this investigation that I had my encounter with the toy wand turning on by itself. Since I discussed this earlier, I won't rehash the story and will continue on with the *"EVP Evidence Summary."*

9:27 P.M.

I recorded the first EVP of the night in the basement before the news team's arrival and believe it proves that ghosts of children haunt the building.

I'm not sure if what I recorded is an audio remnant from the past, or if I recorded evidence of something occurring real time in a parallel realm.

There is not much to explain because what I recorded is a child screaming.

It's hard to tell if it is a boy or a girl. But it sounds like a very young person. Following the scream is the voice of a man saying, *"Quiet."*

The scream is bloodcurdling and even though I wasn't in the basement when it happened, as loud as it was, I should have heard it from anywhere in the building. But I didn't.

Considering what Corinna told her parents about her friend Donald, the lost boy looking for his momma. I'm uncertain if it is him or not, because whoever this child is, seems to have an adult nearby telling them to be quiet.

It doesn't rule out that the voice is Donald's, because it could be a remnant or residual from a time before or after Donald became lost.

10:16 P.M.

There is not much to tell about the second EVP as it is a noise rather than a voice and comes from the basement.

What I recorded is loud and sounds like furniture or something being dragged. It makes a vibrational sound like a heavy desk being slid or moved.

10:31 P.M.

Of all the rooms upstairs, the one that produced the least amount of audio evidence during my five investigations, is what I call the extra room.

Its location is adjacent and south of the children's playroom. The Stocks use it for storage rather than living space. I recorded three EVP's in this room, all on July 3.

It's impossible to know for sure who or what the voices I record refer to when they speak, unless something is said to tie the EVP to the location.

So, I have no way to determine if the next recording is talking about something that happened in the building or not.

I was in the dining room at the far end of the upstairs with the television crew. So, no one was within a hundred feet of the recorder.

What I recorded was a man's voice that says. *"They abuse her!"* Which leads me to believe the voice witnessed whatever took place.

10:35 P.M.

When I recorded the 10:35 P.M. EVP, the television crew, and I were still in the dining room and the only woman in the building was Leslie from Channel 20.

This is important, because the voice I recorded is a woman, who speaks only four minutes after the, *"They abuse her,"* EVP.

She says nothing too substantial, merely saying *"Hello!"*

Based on the tone and tempo of the voice, the *"Hello"* sounds more like she is asking if someone is there, rather than greeting someone.

11:43 P.M.

The next EVP is evidence of an intelligent reply to a question that I asked aloud. It also came from the extra room and was again the voice of a woman.

The television crew left before eleven o'clock, so no one was in the building but me.

While in the room, I decided to asked questions aloud to see if I could coax a response. Out of six questions I asked, there was one response.

The question asked was; *"Do you like Adam and Jessica living here."*

I didn't hear the response, but when I reviewed the audio file from my recorder, sure enough there was a reply. The response was just two seconds after my question and says, *"Live here?"* As if to say, *"You mean someone else lives here.?"*

In addition, the voice sounds very similar to the one recorded at 10:35 P.M. in the extra room that says *"Hello!"*

I had placed the recorder on a wooden box on the northwest side of the room.

The next closest recorder to it was in the children's playroom, which did not pick up either of the voices.

12:31 A.M.

The next piece of evidence recorded adds even further evidence that a child roams the building.

It is a voice recorded in the upstairs hallway on a dresser near the walk-in shower. This is also the area where the shadow man roams.

The voice is that of a child, and what he or she says is heart-rending. Because it is a little voice that says, *"Daddy,"* as if to say, *"Daddy, where are you?"*

The child sounds more like a little boy than a girl, but it's hard to tell. It may or may not be Donald, but it would make sense if Corinna's friend were looking for his mommy, that he is also looking for his daddy.

12:34 A.M.

A second EVP, recorded just three minutes later by the same recorder, is anything but heart-rending.

The voice is male, and I am not sure if it is talking to me or to some invisible phantom. What was said is vulgar, so I have to let you fill in the blanks.

What I recorded is, *"F--- You!"*

This isn't the first time that I have recorded this being said during an investigation. But I was surprised by what I heard. Was it the shadow man that said it? Who knows, but I recorded it near where he roams.

12:52 A.M.

I recorded the next EVP in the laundry area at the southeast corner of the living quarters next to the elevator.

Two things are said and although it sounds like the same person is talking, it also sounds like he is talking to someone else about someone they have been looking for.

The conversation takes up twenty-one seconds. First you hear a male voice say, *"He's right here."* Followed eleven seconds later by the same voice saying, *"He's right here... You staying boy?"*

One can only speculate, but it sounds to me like one or more people were looking for someone and found the party they were searching for and announce they found him to the others.

I assume the party found was a boy, based on the *"You staying boy?"* question.

Taking my speculation further, if Donald was looking for his mommy and daddy, it would make sense that someone was also searching for him. Did I perhaps capture the moment in time that they found him?

12:53 A.M.
It's hard to determine if the next EVP has any relevance to the Dr. Ugs building or its former occupants. I recorded it in the laundry area.

The voice is male and says, *"Fired him."*

My first thought when I heard the voice is that it is referring to someone they dismissed from their job, which makes sense based on all the different businesses housed in the building over the years.

12:54 A.M.
I recorded the last EVP of the night in the girl's bedroom. Again, it was a male voice, only it sounded different from the other male voices recorded during the July 3 investigation.

The voice says, *"Promise him!"*

It's a longshot, but does the voice relate to the James Potter shooting?

Could the voice be Alfred Dodd's, Potter's boss, asking Potter to promise not to show up at the funeral or have any involvement with the funeral arrangements for Davis's family member?

If this is the case. We know how that turned out.

SB-7 Spirit Box Session

11:47 A.M.
I conducted the spirit box session from 11:30 A.M. until 11:50 A.M.

Nothing relevant or clear was coming through and I was about to turn off the device, when I asked if there was a message for anyone.

As soon as I asked, I heard a clear voice, say. *"Yes!"* I could not tell if it was male or female, but it clearly said, *"Yes!"*

So, I asked a follow-up question. Which was? *"Who is the message for?"*

I waited for a response, but only heard static coming through. Then seventeen seconds after I asked the question, a clear male voice responded and said. *"Hayden!"*

You can imagine my surprise when the voice said the name. It was so very clear.

After all, I was in a building where I recorded a dog barking that sounded like it is inside, not once, but on two occasions.

Then come to find out, Jessica has felt a dog jump into bed with her several times. Add to this, the former owners of the building, owned a dog named Hayden killed crossing the street.

Now, I hear the name *"Hayden"* coming through a radio device in the middle of the night. A radio device that scans the frequencies so fast, that clear voices and words should not be possible to receive.

Before delving into the paranormal as an investigator, I believed in fate. But I no longer do. Neither do I think it is a coincidence that a voice said the name Hayden, in a building where a dog by the same name once lived.

I believe in the possibility that the voice that came through either knows Hayden the dog or knew that I was familiar with the name in relation to the building's history.

To me, as an open-minded investigator, the voice saying Hayden offers additional proof that there may be a ghost dog roaming the premises.

EVPs from the Halloween 2018 Investigation

Many believe Halloween is the time of year when the veil between our world and the spirit world is at its thinnest.

As darkness falls and our children travel from door to door seeking treats instead of mischievous deeds, jack-o'-lanterns are lit to celebrate

All Hallows Eve. Intended or not, this reaffirms our connection to the dead.

To some, observing Halloween is controversial and many religions discourage participation, suggesting that celebrating it offers praise to paganism and the occult.

Although this may not be the intent, in a way they are right.

So, is the connection between the living and dead stronger during this time as many believe and offer us a better chance to communicate with the other side?

For me, the jury is still out on this question.

But I will say, some of the strangest things I have seen and best evidence I have gathered, have been on Halloween night.

An example of this occurred on Halloween night 2011 at the haunted Legacy Theatre in Springfield, Illinois.

It was during this investigation that a light in the basement turned on and off on my command.

The light turned on and off, not once, but four times in succession, when I asked it to, and two other investigators saw it.

Earlier in the book, I briefly mentioned a second example of the strangeness that Halloween night offers. It occurred Halloween night of 2016, when I spent the night at Norb Andy's Tavern, a famous watering hole and former morgue, also in Springfield, Illinois.

It was on this night that local television reporter Lindsey Hess, radio personality Chris "Jammer" Neal and the building's owner Todd Gedaminski spent the night with me in the building.

At 4:03 A.M. we all witnessed the jukebox power on by itself and play a song.

What was the name of the song you asked?

It was *"Demons,"* by the band, Imagine Dragons. Not only did we witness this, but we also recorded multiple disembodied voices that night, including an EVP of a little girl singing, *"You're going to hell!"*

You have already read about the EVP recorded in the Dr. Ugs building during my investigation Halloween night of 2017, when I recorded the sound of a gunshot followed by a voice.

It was also on Halloween night 2017 that I recorded the dog barking on multiple recorders.

12:19 A.M.

Halloween night, 2018 would not disappoint, as I recorded the loudest, clearest, EVP I have recorded since investigating the paranormal.

It was while I was in the basement that I recorded it. Of the five recorders upstairs, only one captured the voices, which was, the recorder in the kitchen.

I was over four hours into the audio review when I discovered that I had recorded part of a conversation.

The audio leading up to the EVP was silence, other than hearing an occasional car pass by.

Then, out of nowhere, a woman speaks. She asks the question.

"Is that motorized?"

Following her voice is that of a young boy who answers by responding, *"Hell Yeah!"* Followed again by silence.

It sounded like a conversation between two living people in the same room as me, except no one else was in the building.

The quality of the recording is the Holy Grail of EVP's and is the best I ever recorded. The verbalization is clear, so there was no need to enhance the volume or remove white noise from the background.

Based on the woman's question, my guess is, I recorded a conversation that took place between 1910 and the 1960s, when the word motorized was more common.

The tone of the boy's response seems to suggest he is proud of having a motorized device.

When I replayed the audio clip for Adam and Jessica, it stunned them as much as it did me, due to the vociferous clarity of the voices. It was as if two people were standing in the kitchen, carrying on a conversation.

We discussed the possibility that the voice of the woman could be the same voice Adam and Corinna heard talking to Ella, as she walked out of the kitchen in December 2018, but Adam was not sure.

12:58 A.M.

12:58 A.M., was the last piece of evidence recorded during the investigation.

When I first listened to it, I thought what I heard was someone hiccupping followed a second later by a loud bang as if something was dropped

I neither hiccupped nor dropped anything during the investigation. This I can assure you of.

As I do with all EVPs, I listened to the audio clip multiple times. At one point I heard something different.

I noticed how close that the bang sounded to the gunshot EVP I recorded just one year before on Halloween night of 2017.

Then I realized that the hiccup portion of the EVP also sounds like a gasp.

I played the EVP sequence over and over. As I did, I noticed how the first part of the clip; the gasp sounds like the breath being taken away from someone, moments before experiencing a frightening event, such as being shot.

So, rather than recording a hiccup and simple bang, did I again record the sound of someone being shot, on Halloween night?

When I compared the gunshot from the 2017 investigation with the EVP, other than the volume being louder from 2017, they sound very similar.

Unlike the gunshot EVP from 2017, I didn't have the luxury of having a voice say, *"shot him,"* during the audio sequence to offer additional evidence that the recording is of a ghostly gunshot.

So, the only thing I am sure of about what is taking place during the 12:58 EVP sequence, is that it is interesting, but what happened is inconclusive.

The rest of the investigation was uneventful, with nothing seen, heard or recorded. But as the old saying goes, *"It's about quality, not quantity."* And the conversation between the woman and boy, was definitely high-quality evidence.

EVPs from the April 2019 Investigation

10:00 P.M.

Since putting pen to paper to write this book, the April 2019 investigation is the last I have conducted at Dr. Ugs. Based on evidence I have collected since first investigating the building in 2017, I'm sure there will be more investigations to come.

Each of the first four investigations proved fruitful and the April 17 investigation was no different as I recorded eight clear EVP's.

The weather forecast showed thunderstorms later in the night. Many paranormal enthusiasts believe that the electrical discharge caused by lightening, energize the atmosphere making for the perfect storm for ghosts.

I'm not sure if this was the case during the investigation, as most of the evidence I recorded occurred before the thunderstorms.

I recorded the first EVP at 10:00 P.M. Only a recorder on the dresser in the hallway where Adam and Jessica have seen the shadow man recorded it.

Once again, none of the other nearby recorders captured the voice, which, from a technical standpoint, makes little sense.

I was standing between the east hallway and the playroom. I asked a random question, trying to coax a verbal response.

At 10:00 P.M. I ask the following question. *"If the little boy is here. Can you play with the toys so I can hear you playing?"*

Soon after asking, I recorded a voice that says. *"No."*

The voice was faint. When I enhanced the volume of the EVP, I could hear the *"no"* response but could not determine if it is male or female or if it is a child or an adult.

10:54 P.M.
The recorder on the hallway dresser also captured the second EVP of the night.

I rate it as one of the more chilling voices that I have recorded since I began my journey as a paranormal investigator.

The tone of the voice is best described as a gruff or growling voice and is something I would expect to find at places where negative type activity takes place and not at a place like Dr. Ugs.

The voice says.

"Lucifer!"

My concern when I heard the voice was whether it was a benevolent spirit saying the name or talking about Lucifer, or if I recorded a malevolent supernatural being of a lower negative existence.

The activity that the Stock family has experienced at the Virginia location has so far been of the benign nature.

This makes me wonder if the voice is a spirit or supernatural being that I have encountered over the years at another location, who may have no connection to the Dr. Ugs haunting and may have showed up to pay me a visit.

If you are not sure what I am referring to and have not read my books, *"Chasing Shadows or Where Evil Lurks,"* you should do so as they go into detail discussing my experience with negative activity associated with a particular location.

So, is the voice connected to the building or me? I don't know.

My gut feeling tells me that the voice is more associated with me and wanted me to hear it. But as I have learned over the years, no one knows the answers to the questions that the supernatural bestows to us.

10:56 P.M.

The next EVP was captured in the playroom. Even though there were three other recorders all within twenty-five feet of the recorder in the playroom, only one recorded the EVP.

It may be a bit of a stretch, but what the voice says could relate to the ghost dog that seems to wander about the building.

The voice was male and says.

"I walked it!"

The *"it,"* portion of the EVP could refer to many things, including a child, a horse, a dog, etc. But a dog is certainly one possibility.

When recording random disembodied voices, there are so many unanswered questions about them.

It makes little sense that spirits or ethereal beings would wander about spewing random words. So, is our equipment only picking up bits and pieces of conversations? I believe this is the case.

If we consider how the SB-7 spirit box works, scanning multiple frequencies in a short amount of time and how even though it shouldn't be able to. It not only picks up words, but complete sentences that come from the same voice.

When you listen to a radio station and the announcer says, *"You are listening to 99.7,"* what the announcer means is that you are listening to a radio station broadcasting an FM radio signal at a frequency of 99.7 megahertz. Megahertz is measured in millions of cycles per second.

This means that the stations transmitter is oscillating at 99,700,000 cycles per second.

So, when you tune the radio dial to the specific frequency of 99.7, if your radio is in range, it will pick up the signal.

Every microphone and every speaker has a frequency range that it picks up. For example, when you are trying to pick out the best microphone to record a certain instrument, you need to know the frequency range of the mic and the range of the instrument.

My theory is that the disembodied voices that we pick up, for whatever reason, use some frequencies in the sound spectrum of our world, but also use frequencies that we cannot detect and the audio recorders we use cannot detect either.

So, much of what they say goes undetected. But if we allow our recorders to record for long periods of time like I do on investigations, which is eight hours or more, the odds of picking up a voice coming through on a frequency that we can detect increases and we record some of what they say.

11:37 P.M.

The next EVP is a voice loud enough to hear, but difficult to understand. I picked the voice up on my recorder in the children's bedroom.

It is a male voice, and either says, *"Wait and see,"* or *"urgency."*

Not understanding what a disembodied voice is saying is common in paranormal investigating. Many times, white noise hides the voices and other times the entities accent makes it difficult to understand what they are saying. It is not uncommon that two people listening to the same EVP will hear something different.

Many of the EVP's I recorded in the five investigations at Dr. Ugs were clear and are what are call, *"Class A,"* EVP's in paranormal investigating lingo.

I can't take credit for the term, because I first heard it used in 2009 on the television show, Ghost Lab. It's another way of saying that an EVP is high quality.

The voice, in this case, is not clear enough to guess what it was talking about or whether it applies to the building.

12:15 A.M.

At 12:15 A.M., I recorded an EVP on two different recorders.

It was recorded in the children's and Adam and Jessica's bedroom, which are next to each other.

The voice says, *"Hello!"*

One could say that "Hello" was not for anyone specific and was something my recorder picked up coming from another realm of existence and has nothing to do with me or the building.

But if you go with logic, since I was the only person in the building, whoever is talking, is probably talking to me.

The word hello is one of the more frequent words I have recorded on investigations.

I believe the entities that paranormal investigators record know we are trying to record them, so they call out to us.

I also believe that somehow, they know the location where we will be and show up or access our realm to communicate with us.

12:30 A.M.
The next EVP that I recorded sounds like part of a conversation between a man and a woman.

I'm not sure if the conversation is friendly teasing or if the woman is scolding the man for being a shyster. I recorded the conversation in the playroom.

First you hear the woman say or declare, *"You rat!"* Followed by the man declaring, *"I sold shit!"* Both voices are clear, so there is no doubt what they say.

The building has been home to many businesses, so I'm sure merchants had their share of dissatisfied customers.

When I heard the exchange, it sounded like the woman was an angry customer proclaiming her disgust with the man.

The man saying, *"I sold shit!"* Sounds like he is proclaiming, *"Yes, you are right."*

Recording disembodied voices interacting with each other is rare in my experience. But during the five investigations at Dr. Ugs, I recorded three examples of this.

One, we just discussed, the second is the woman asking, *"Is that motorized"* and the third, is the EVP we are about to discuss.

4:49 A.M.
I talked about the next EVP earlier in the book, but I will discuss it here in more detail.

I mentioned that I recorded a dog barking that sounded like it was coming from within the building for a second time.

If you will recall, the first time that I recorded barking was during the Halloween night 2017 investigation.

Making the April 2019 recording even more interesting, following the barking, a man with a gruff voice speaks, then the dog barks again.

Although what he says is a little distorted, you can hear the man say, *"dog."* Then say what sounds like, *"lay down."*

The man speaks as soon as the dog barks, so more than likely, he is interacting with the animal.

I had multiple recorders placed upstairs, but the only recorder to capture the sound of the dog and voice of the man was my recorder in the playroom.

The barking dog recorded in October 2017 and April 2019 are both loud and echo, like they are coming from inside the building. Even more important, the barking sounds like it is the same dog.

Weighing the Evidence

Now with the story of my investigation nearing its end. It's time to sift through the evidence and compare what I found with the eyewitness accounts of the strange things that take place.

In doing so, I hope to confirm that the unusual activity Adam and Jessica Stock experienced at 142 East Beardstown Street, is real, ghostly in nature and ongoing.

Paranormal investigations are like the investigations I conducted as a private investigator; except I stake out the dead instead of the living.

Over a period of eighteen months, I spent more than forty hours alone in the building, surveilling, and conducting my investigation into the strange events that take place at Dr. Ugs.

By going alone, I free myself from influence and bias that others might cause and eliminate the possibility of recording the voice of someone accompanying me and mistaking their voice for legitimate paranormal evidence.

Besides my experiences and observations, I have interviewed the Stocks and others, who have witnessed firsthand, the mystery that takes place.

All the witnesses I interviewed were credible and I believe their stories.

I hope by comparing the evidence that I gathered with the eyewitness accounts of others, the picture that is the haunting of Dr. Ugs, will become clearer.

With this being said, there are many questions related to the haunting that remain unanswered. But in the grand scheme of things, we may be better off not knowing what the answers are.

I have concluded that it doesn't matter how many hours or years that I investigate the supernatural or how much evidence that I get, because I will never unravel the mysteries of the supernatural.

These are God's secrets and until He is ready to reveal the answers to us, the mysteries will remain unsolved.

The EVP evidence I recorded in the building is substantial. Much more than I have recorded at any location since becoming a paranormal investigator.

I am not sure why this is, but somehow, the veil to the other side is thinner in the Dr. Ugs building then it is at most places.

As I summarize the evidence for you, you will see why paranormal mysteries are so hard to solve and why questions go unanswered.

But as I have found out, when investigating the supernatural, unanswered questions are the nature of the beast.

I will do my best to show how the evidence I collected correlates with the experiences the Stock's and others have had. By doing this, I hope to unravel at least some of the mystery for you.

Who haunts the building?

Based on eyewitness accounts and the evidence that I have obtained in the form of EVP's, at least, five ghosts haunt the building.

A small boy, two adult males, an adult woman and a ghost dog.

But because of differences in tone and tempo of the voices I recorded, I believe there may be several children and additional adults haunting the building.

So, who are they?

Ghost Children

As you will recall, there are four eyewitness accounts of ghost children haunting the building.

The first account took place when Adam and Jessica overheard their daughter Corinna talking while playing alone. It didn't sound like gibberish but sounded as if she was conversing with someone.

Corinna was two and a half and just learning how to talk. Her parents had never heard her speak in sentences as she did that afternoon.

Based on Adam and Jessica's questioning of Corinna, we know that she was talking to a little boy named Donald, who sucks his fingers and is looking for his mama.

A second encounter with a little boy occurred in the restaurant kitchen in 2013, when a cook witnessed the incident.

The cook was adamant that he saw a little boy running around the kitchen one morning. Thinking it was the Stocks child, you can imagine his surprise when he told Jessica that her little boy was running around the kitchen and she informed him she didn't have a little boy.

Jessica didn't get a description of the boy from the cook and he no longer works for the Stocks, so we do not know what he looks like.

The third incident with a phantom child occurred January 2, 2017 when a friend and colleague of mine, Scott McCullar attended a wedding reception at Dr. Ugs. His encounter, although not visual, was chilling.

If you will recall, Scott needed to use the men's room, but when he approached it, he heard giggling and the voices of children inside the bathroom.

He waited, but when his wait became too long, he jiggled the doorknob and opened the door, finding the room empty.

I witnessed a fourth event that may be further proof of a child phantom haunting the building on April 17, 2019. This is when I saw the short silhouette of a person blocking the view of my camera.

Although the shadowy figure had no identifiable features, I can't rule out the possibility it was a child because of its short stature.

The physical evidence that I recorded is just as intriguing as the eyewitness accounts and stories.

I recorded the first two pieces of evidence of children in the building on the same night. July 3, 2018. One EVP was recorded in the basement and one upstairs in the east hallway.

The first EVP recorded at 9:27 P.M. is disturbing.

It is disturbing because it is of a screaming child, who screams not once but screams two times.

After the screams, you can hear the voice of a man say *"Quiet,"* as if he is scolding the child to stop screaming.

After listening to it, I got the impression that what I recorded is a child being disciplined.

I recorded the second EVP of a child that night at 12:31 A.M. The voice calls out, *"Daddy!"* Based on the tone and tempo of the voice, it sounds like the child is looking for their parent.

The two clips are children, but I can't determine their gender based on the recordings. They both sound very young. So, it is possible that one or both EVP's could be Donald.

I recorded the third voice of a child on Halloween night 2018. It is one of my favorite EVP's of all time because it is so clear and is a conversation between two people.

The quality of the clip gives you the feeling you are in the same room with them and maybe I was.

First, a woman asks, *"Is that motorized?"* Followed by the voice of a boy who replies, *"Hell yeah!"*

No doubt the voice responding, *"Hell yeah,"* is male. But he sounds much older than the young boy Donald, that Corrina described.

Based on the sound of the voice, my guess is that he is at least ten years old, if not older.

The voice of the child saying *"Daddy,"* could be the same as the child's scream but is not the same as the voice saying, *"Hell yeah."*

This evidence seems to confirm that Donald is not the only ghost child in the building and that there are at least two, if not more. That is unless I recorded the same child during two different ages in his life.

Male Ghosts

Only one person has seen male ghosts in the building, which is Jessica. She has seen a shadow man twice and the man in the mirror several times.

Adam witnessed the shadowy figure long enough to tell someone was there. But not long enough to determine its gender.

The phantom that Jessica encountered appeared different each time she saw it. *"I'm not sure if they are the same ghost. But I feel they are connected to each other."* Jessica said.

In her first encounter, the phantom appeared as a dark figure; about the same height as Adam, with broader shoulders. Not transparent like a ghost, but more solid in appearance and what she saw was dressed in all black. He wore a long flowing high collar black coat that draped over his body.

The second time Jessica witnessed the shadow man, he looked different. Unlike her first encounter, he was white in appearance, with a white collar and wearing what looked like an old fashion top hat, also white.

"His face was unclear. But it was definitely a man." Jessica said.

If the shadow men are the same. We must ask the question. Do ghost change clothes as we do? Or are they seen wearing clothes that correlate to a particular event or time period?

The second and or third male specter witnessed by Jessica is the man in the mirror.

His description differs from the two shadow men. The shadow figures are similar in size to Adam, who is of medium height. The man in the mirror is a large man.

Plus, the shadow men are only seen upstairs and the man in the mirror downstairs.

So, based on eyewitness accounts, we have one man who is medium height, black and shadowy in appearance. One who is medium height, white and shadowy in appearance and one who is large with light-colored hair and ghostly in appearance.

The best we can surmise based on the visual sighting evidence is that there are two or maybe three phantom men roaming the building.

But what does our audio evidence tell us about this?

Although I recorded many EVPs during the five investigations. There are seventeen that are male voices.

To determine the number of different male voices recorded. I did a comparison study of the seventeen EVPs using audio editing software. I compared tone, pitch and tempo and also listened for similar sounding accents.

The results fall into three categories:
Inconclusive–Either distorted, or the volume was too faint for comparison.
Unique–No other voices were similar.
Unique but similar–Groupings of similar voices, different from other groups and unique voices.

Inconclusive–Of the seventeen, the results for three EVPs were inconclusive.

Those are, "Wait *and see or Urgency*" recorded April 2019, *"Hello"* recorded April 2019 and *"I will say"* recorded April 2018.

Unique–The results of four voices recorded are unique from the others.

Those are, *"Shot him"* recorded October 2017, *"Promise him"* recorded July 2018, *"Lucifer"* recorded April 2019 and *"I sold shit"* recorded April 2019.

Unique but similar–There were three clusters of EVPs falling into this category.
((Cluster one)
"Hit wall" recorded on October 2017 and *"Wall is Hidden"* recorded April 2018. These two EVPs sound like the same spirit or entity and both mention a wall.

(Cluster two)
"Hey" recorded April 2018, *"Quiet"* recorded after the child's scream on July 2018 and *"Dog"* recorded after the dog barking April 2019. The three EVPs sound like the same spirit or entity.

(Cluster three)

"*They abuse her,*" recorded July 2018, "*F—k you*" recorded July 2018, "*He's right here. You staying boy*" recorded July 2018, "*Fired him*" recorded July 2018 and "*I walked it,*" recorded April 2019, all sound like the same voice.

So, what the audio analysis of male voices shows, is four voices differ from other EVPs and three clusters of similar sounding voices differ from the four unique voices which leaves us with the possibility of seven different male voices recorded in the five investigations.

If we factor in knowing there are at least two different children in the building, combined with the possibility of seven or more adult male spirits, we can surmise that there are no fewer than nine spirits haunting the building.

But alas, we are not finished with our analysis as we still have to account for females and ghost animals.

Female Ghosts

Although no one has witnessed a female ghost in the building. Adam and Corinna both heard a woman's voice in December 2018.

Of all the EVPs I recorded during my five investigations, only three were female. Those were, "*Live here,*" recorded July 2018, "*Is that motorized,*" recorded October 2018 and, "*You rat,*" recorded April 2019.

When I did a similar audio analysis of female voices, as I did with male voices, none sounded similar.

I also played the voices for Adam, but he wasn't sure if any sounded like the voice of the woman he overheard talking to his daughter Ella.

We know based on what Corinna told her parents, that Donald, the ghost boy, is looking for his mother. So, it is possible that one of the female voices I recorded is Donald's mother.

Psychic Evidence

In April 2019, I contacted a friend in Atchison, Kansas, who has psychic abilities. If you have read two of my previous books, *"Chasing Shadows and Dark Creepy Places"* you have read about him before.

His name is Tony, and although he is very gifted, he doesn't do readings, nor does he want to be labeled as a psychic for personal reasons.

I have seen him in action many times and am convinced his abilities are real.

For this reason, I sent him several photos to look at from the Dr. Ugs building to see if he could pick up on anything related to the building.

I didn't tell him anything about the building, where it is located or what was taking place. I merely sent the photos and asked him if he picked up on any spirit activity.

Here is the response that I received from Tony.

"Hey Larry, from looking at the photos, I can tell you there is a very curious little boy spirit. He is curious of the children who live there now. Along with the boy spirit is a woman, I feel his mother, she is very protective of the boy and is almost jealous of the time he likes to watch the family. Her feelings of uneasiness make her energy higher so this could explain why the little girl sees her. I hope that makes sense."

"I feel they left this world either at the same time or very close to each other. When you are there, focus a lot of your time on the little girl's room. I pick up on the woman and a little boy veering into the room from the hall. The boy is attracted to the family's little girl, out of curiosity. Also, there is a dark wardrobe in a few of your photos. I'd be curious of its history. Feels like this woman's energy is around it a lot but cannot tell if it's because she owned it at one time or is just attracted to it, because it reminds her of one, she owned. There's also a photo of a lot of toys in a room? I feel the boy visits this room often, so it might be a good spot to catch something."

When I received Tony's message, it flabbergasted me for several reasons. First, Tony didn't know who lived in the building. So, he could not have known that the Stocks have children, let alone know they have girls.

But in his message, he said the woman's feelings of uneasiness made her energy higher, allowing the little girl to see her. So, if Ella sees and talks to a phantom woman, this helps to explain why she can see her.

He also mentioned how the little boy is attracted to the family's little girl. Which may explain Corina's conversation with Donald.

Tony alluded to how the little boy often visits the room with toys. If he is correct, and the phantom boy plays with the toys.

This would explain why the Stocks hear toys operating on their own.

After receiving Tony's first message, I sent him several EVPs to listen to, including the one that sounds like a gunshot followed by the man's voice saying, *"Shot him."*

Here is Tony's reply after listening to the EVPs.

Larry, the EVP is a gunshot, what's the history? I ask this because I'm picking up this woman hates to leave the boys side. Like she lost him once and will not do it again, I'm wondering if he died from an illness and she took her life, because she couldn't bear to be without him. I'm not picking up any names, sorry, wish I was, but I'm not. I'm also not at this point picking up on a husband.

Based on the woman's voice that Adam heard, the three EVPs I recorded and Tony's clairvoyant insight, I am convinced there is at least one and maybe more female spirits haunting the Dr. Ugs building.

I hope that further investigations I conduct will add additional evidence to confirm this.

Ghost Dog

The most compelling evidence that a ghost dog haunts the building. Is not just finding the EVP of a dog barking that sounds like it is inside the building. But that I found it, before Adam told me that something that feels like a dog jumping into bed, wakes Jessica in the middle of the night.

Not to mention the barking echoes and sounds like it comes from inside the building.

I recorded the barking on four recorders, enabling me to triangulate where it was coming from. Which is the upstairs kitchen in the living quarters.

To top it off, when I interviewed the previous owners of the building, Mike and Susan Carson. I found out they had a pet dog named Hayden, who lived with them, but died after being hit by a car crossing the street.

The Carson's told me that even after Hayden's death. They continued to hear his dog tags jingling in the building and in the back seat of their car.

During my last investigation April 2019, I recorded the sound of a dog barking again. Only this time, besides the barking, I recorded a man's voice that sounds like he is scolding the dog.

The barking from the April 2019 investigation was as loud as the EVP I recorded in October 2017, but was only picked up by one recorder, which made little sense.

I have recorded dogs barking on many investigations in the last nineteen years. But I can always tell that they come from outdoors. As a matter of fact, I recorded a dog barking during one investigation while at Dr. Ugs, that was identifiable as coming from the outside.

The barking EVPs recorded on October 2017 and April 2019 were loud and echoed, convincing me they came from within the building.

Add to this, the spirit box session where a voice called out the name Hayden.

So, the preponderance of evidence points that not only do the ghost of people haunt the building, but so does a phantom canine. Unfortunately, what the evidence cannot determine is how many ghostly entities there are.

Like the old saying goes, *"If you don't have the numbers to add, you can hardly figure a sum."*

Epilogue

When friend and former baseball teammate Bob Roodhouse told me that his nephew lived in a haunted building. Never in my wildest dreams did I expect to find a place so shrouded in mystery.

Nor did I expect to record the amount of indisputable evidence that I captured during my investigations. Investigations that I conducted alone, in a controlled environment.

By investigating alone, I can say with certainty that what I recorded is genuine, unexplained, paranormal evidence of a haunting taking place at 142 East Beardstown Street, Virginia, Illinois.

But, instead of answering questions, my evidence has led to more of them. It does offer reassurance for Adam and Jessica, that they are not imagining the ghostly things they experienced. Nor were their employees or my friend Scott McCullar.

If I have learned anything during my years as a paranormal investigator. It is that we cannot define hauntings as a single phenomenon. Because each is unique having its own cast of characters and storyline.

If you were to write a screenplay about the Dr. Ugs haunting, based on eyewitness accounts and the evidence, at a minimum, you would have to include the following characters in your script.

"Donald the Ghost Boy, The Shadow Man, A Woman, The Man in the Mirror, The Man with the Gruff voice and a Ghost Dog."

But if we could lift the veil and see what goes on behind the scenes, I believe the list of characters would be much longer and my evidence agrees. I venture to say there is at least one other woman and several men and children haunting the building

There are those who claim that this or that location is the most haunted place in existence. Or they create *"Top Ten"* list of the most haunted places.

I'm not sure how they measure such claims, but I would be more agreeable with them if their claim was, *"This is the most haunted place I have been, so far."*

If Dr. Ugs is not the most haunted place I have investigated, it is near the top of my list. A list that includes places like the Villisca Ax Murder House and Farrar School in Iowa, Ridge Cemetery at Williamsburg Hill and Norb Andy's Tavern in Illinois and Rockcliffe Mansion in Missouri.

But I can say, without doubt, the Dr. Ugs building in Virginia, is the number one location I have investigated, for recording disembodied voices known as *Electronic Voice Phenomena.*

One piece of evidence I recorded Halloween night of 2017, is likely connected to a tragic event that occurred in 1929. I am referring to the EVP of a loud gunshot followed by the voice of a man saying, *"Shot him!"*

If it does relate to the James Potter shooting. Then what did I record?

Was it the actual event taking place through some time warp? Do spirits re-create or mimic the sounds of events they experienced while living? Or is an earthbound ghost, so haunted by his or her guilt, that their memory of what happened years ago, is detectible by my recording equipment?

Is the little boy the cook saw, the children's voices Scott McCullar heard, the child screaming and the child calling out, *"Daddy,"* that I recorded, Corinna's playmate Donald?

What about the conversation between the woman and the young boy? The woman sounded impressed by something she was seeing when she asked, *"Is that motorized?"* And the boy sounded a little braggadocio when he replied, *"Hell yeah!"*

Then there is the woman with a different sounding voice that says, *"You rat,"* followed by a man saying, *"I sold shit!"*

With the multitude of men's voices recorded, much like the old cliché, *"It's difficult to tell the players without a scorecard."*

So, if you are wondering how many male ghosts are in the building. I don't have an answer for you, other than I believe the number ranges from several to many.

I will say, based on the descriptions of the two shadow men that Jessica saw upstairs and the man in the mirror downstairs. There are at least three.

Just when I thought I had seen it all in my days as a paranormal investigator, I encountered a phenomenon I had read about, but had never experienced. Ghost animals.

Recording the dog barking is one thing. But what I recorded is loud and echoes, as though it comes from within the building. By triangulating the barking based on the intensity of the recorded sound, I was able to determine that the barking emanated from the upstairs kitchen.

Even more interesting, is that when I recorded it, I didn't know about Jessica's encounters with what feels like a dog jumping into bed with her.

Although the Dr. Ugs haunting remains shrouded in mystery. There are two things that I learned based on my investigations.

Which are, reality is more complicated than it might seem, and ethereal things exist that can be seen and heard, but not explained.

After investigating the Dr. Ugs building, one thing is certain. I will soon be back on the case, hanging out in the dark corridors of 142 East Beardstown Street, hoping to unravel some of the mystery behind the Dr. Ugs haunting.

As Lawrence Dobkin, the narrator of the 1950s television series, *The Naked City*, would say each week.

"There are eight million stories in the naked city; this has been one of them."

And what a story it is.

Happy Hauntings!

Larry Wilson

Campfire Tales Extra

From the Author

Dr. Ugs, *"A Haunting in Virginia, Illinois,"* is the first in a new series of books called *"Campfire Tales,"* published by Chiller Books.

Being a paranormal investigator who also writes books. I do a lot of book signing events throughout the Midwest.

During the events, I meet an array of folks who not only come to buy books but come to share stories of their encounters with the mysterious and the unexplained.

As an added feature, each book in the *"Campfire Tales,"* series will include a section called, "Paranormal Witness." Which will allow me to share some of the stories of the encounters of others as told to me.

Never in my wildest dreams did I expect I only needed to travel as far as my neighborhood in Taylorville, Illinois, to find the tales I was looking for.

Even more unexpected, is the first story of the series, was told to me by neighbor and friend Tim Zini, who was my son's junior high school history teacher and very well respected in the community.

So, credit for the chilling stories you are about to read goes to Mr. Tim Zini of Taylorville, Illinois.

Paranormal Witness

STRANGERS IN THE NIGHT

Tim Zini

The story you are about to read is true and happened in the fall of 1980 or 1981.

I was living in Edinburg, Illinois and worked in the maintenance department at the Commonwealth Edison power plant on route 104 near Kincaid, Illinois.

I do not recall the exact date, but it was between the middle of October and Thanksgiving. The weather was chilly, but not cold. I was working the 11:00 P.M. to 8:00 A.M. shift.

To get from my house to the power plant, I traveled the Kincaid-Edinburg blacktop.

The blacktop is a shortcut through the countryside ending at route 104, in the Village of Bulpit.

It is a winding road with many hills to go up and down. It was pitch black, and I was driving with my high beam lights on to see where I was going.

As I headed down one hill, I noticed that someone was standing along the side of the road. When I got closer, I could see that it was a woman.

She was standing in the loose gravel at the side of the road and was staring directly at me. Not at my truck, but at me! I could tell because our eyes met.

The woman was not dressed like someone from the 1980s, but more like you would expect someone from the 1920s to be dressed.

She had a scarf tied around her head and was wearing a three-quarter length coat, and she was not alone. Standing in front of the woman was a young boy who appeared to be nine or ten years old.

His clothes also looked out of place, like they were from another time period. The boy was wearing a long coat and was wearing a flat, wide style cap. A style that you would expect to see a newspaper boy in the 1920s wear.

The woman's arms were around the boy's chest, holding him close to her.

They were both staring at me through the glare of my headlights. Once again, I stress that they were not staring toward me, but at me.

I will never forget their eyes as they were not normal looking but were black like pieces of coal.

They did not move as I passed by them and seemed oblivious to my truck as I sped past, barely missing them.

If you wonder why I didn't stop to see if they needed help, it is because of my dad, who worked the night shift for years for the coal mine and told me over and over of the dangers of the country at night.

He told stories of modern-day highway men who would use women and children as decoys to get good Samaritans to stop so they could rob the unsuspecting traveler.

There were no cars on the side of the road or nearby houses where they could have come from. So, I continued my trip to work.

When I pulled into the parking lot at work. A young man who worked at the power plant came running to my truck.

He was driving into work that night and was following me down the blacktop.

When I opened my truck door to get out, he was there waiting for me.

"What the hell was that Zini?" He asked.

I told him I didn't know, but I would tell Dwight Folkers the shift supervisor.

When I told Folkers what I had seen, he called the county sheriff's department.

Two deputies responded in separate cars. One came east from Edinburg and the other came from the west from Kincaid.

The pair drove toward each other on the blacktop and neither found anyone on the road.

I'm not sure what I saw that night or if I saw something that I shouldn't have. But they looked like two people lost in time.

I know they were there, because the other guy saw them too.

Even though it was forty years ago, when I drive down the blacktop, I think about that night and wonder who or what I saw and what would have happened if I had stopped.

To this day, the hair stands up on the back of my neck when I think about it.

THE HOUSE ON BIG BEND ROAD

Tim Zini

I married my current wife Lisa in 2005, nine years after my first wife passed from illness. Lisa had three boys, and I had one.

Her oldest son was out of the house by the time we married, so living in the house with Lisa and I were her two boys, Jeff and John and my son Alex.

Lisa's youngest son John died in a single car accident his freshman year in college. He died on March 15, the *"Ides of March."*

He lost control of his van and hit the only tree for quite a distance in any direction.

Not long after his death, odd things happened.

After the funeral, we had a house full of friends and relatives. Under the circumstances, there were just too many people and Lisa needed to get away. So, she stepped outside with her sons, Jeff and Ryan to be alone.

They were sitting in a circle, Indian style when a strange yellow bird resembling a canary landed on Ryan's head. The normal reaction would have been to swat the bird away. But Ryan didn't.

The bird just sat there, and so did Ryan. It sat for such a long time that Jeff took several photos and a video with his cell phone. It was like it was Ryan's pet.

We had never seen a bird like this in the neighborhood, either before or since that day and it convince the family that it was John saying goodbye.

On an occasion before John's death, he discussed whether a person could assume the body of an animal after they passed, to be close to loved ones. Maybe he was sharing the answer with us.

After the incident with the bird, strange things began happening inside the house.

I have a Chicago Cubs floppy hat or what some would call a fishing hat. The hat was always nearby because I wore it a lot.

One day, I wanted to wear it, but when I went to retrieve it, it was missing. Lisa and I looked everywhere for it but couldn't find it. It remained missing for weeks.

Then one Saturday morning, Lisa called out for me to come downstairs.

We have a finished basement with carpeting, furniture, a television and an exercise area. When I went downstairs, lying in the middle of the floor between the couch and the television was the hat.

"Oh, you found it!" I said. *"No, it was just there,"* replied Lisa.

Lisa vacuums every Saturday. So, there is no way it could have laid there for a month or more without one of us finding it. The hat disappearing and then showing up out of thin air, was disturbing to Lisa. Because she knew, as I did, that someone had to put it there.

About a month later, the hat disappeared again and as of the writing of this story we have not found it.

Not long ago an equally puzzling event took place. Lisa and I are the only ones living in the house now as the boys are out on their own.

We were in the backyard sitting around our outdoor fireplace looking toward the house, when the silhouette of a person walked past our kitchen window. Lisa and I both saw it and said, *"There's someone in the house!"*

I went inside to check the house, expecting to find an intruder, but all I found was an empty house. No one was there, and the doors and windows were still locked.

Lisa and I are certain that we saw someone in the house that night, so who was the mysterious intruder and where did they go?

A more important question may be, what was the reason for their visit, and will they be back?

THE VILLA ROAD HOUSE

Tim Zini

My first wife and I moved into a house on Villa Road in Edinburg in the early 1980s. It was an exciting time for us the day we moved in. It was just my first wife and I, so we had the house all to ourselves. Or so we thought.

The first few weeks that we lived there, things were a little strange. We would-be lying-in bed trying to sleep and would hear what sounded like we had left the television on. I would get up to see if there was something that I needed to turn off, but nothing would be on Other times, we would hear what sounded like someone carrying on a conversation down the hallway and when I would check it out, no one was there.

It was strange, because when I would enter the living room, it sounded like the noise was coming from the kitchen. When I would go to the kitchen, it sounded like the noise was coming from downstairs.

Eventually, I had my wife check it out with me because she could hear it too. But we could never find the source.

After living in the house for a few weeks, the noise stopped.

Several other strange things happened while living in the house.

I decided to get my teaching degree, which required going back to school. In order to take the classes that I needed, I had to work the midnight shift at the powerplant which meant sleeping during the day.

Many times, I was alone in the house when sleeping and it would be during these times that something would wake me out of a sound sleep.

The first incident that happened was when I was roused out of a sound sleep by heavy breathing right next to me. A second incident which was equally as chilling, occurred when I was shaken awake by an unseen hand. The final circumstance occurred when I was forcibly poked in the hip and startled awake.

I not sure why the activity stopped, but we concluded that who or whatever was in the house was not ready to have someone new in the house, but eventually figured that we were not leaving, so they accepted us and decided to leave us alone.

ABOUT THE AUTHOR

Larry Wilson spent a decade working as a private investigator, before turning his attention to the paranormal. He is the founder of Urban Paranormal Investigations in Central Illinois. In addition to investigating hundreds of locations throughout the Midwest, he is a "Best Selling Author" who has written several books on the topic, guest lectured and has appeared on both television and radio programs.

He is founder of 11:11 Films, an independent film company that produces paranormal documentaries. Larry has also assisted in the filming of three paranormal documentaries for other independent film companies.

Wilson currently resides in Taylorville, Illinois with his wife Kathy.

For more information, please visit:
http://lwilsonurbanparanormalblogspot.com/

Like us on Facebook:
https://www.facebook.com/Urban-Paranormal-Investigations-327088597440791/

Photo by Kathy Wilson

BOOKS BY LARRY WILSON

Chasing Shadows
Echoes from the Grave
Dark Creepy Places
Where Evil Lurks
Dr. Ugs

www.ingramcontent.com/pod-product-compliance
Lightning Source LLC
LaVergne TN
LVHW051502070426
835507LV00022B/2889